NEW YORK

COOK BOOK

Cooking Across America
Cookbook Collection™

GOLDEN WEST ☼
PUBLISHERS

Contributing editors:
Jean Miller Dean and Janice Therese Mancuso

The Kosher Gourmet Cookbook recipes courtesy:
The Kosher Gourmet Cookbook
by the 92nd Street Y Cooking School
1395 Lexington Ave.
New York, NY 10128
(212) 415-5607

Printed in the United States of America

ISBN #1-885590-30-X

3rd Printing © 2003

Golden West Publishers, Inc.
4113 N. Longview Ave.
Phoenix, AZ 85014, USA
(800) 658-5830

Visit our website: http://www.goldenwestpublishers.com

★ ★ ★ ★ *New York Cook Book* ★ ★ ★ ★

Table of Contents

★ ★ ★ ★ *Cooking Across America* ★ ★ ★ ★

Table of Contents (continued)

Introduction

For more than one hundred years the Statue of Liberty has welcomed hopeful travelers to America. Millions of people have settled on these shores and throughout the state of New York, intent on creating new lives and finding their place in this better land. These citizens of the world brought with them rich traditions that have been passed down from one generation to another.

New Yorkers are proud of their state and their heritage and it shows in the variety of fabulous foods presented in these pages. Upstate New York and New York City are well-represented in this cookbook. Filled with traditional favorites like *New York Cheesecake, Buffalo Wings, Spiedie Sandwiches, New York City Knish, Matzo Ball Soup, Coney Island Hot Dogs, Pasta Fagioli, Apple Pie* and many more, **New York Cook Book** will be a treasured keepsake of your time in New York.

Created as part of the *Cooking Across America Cookbook Collection*, the recipes in **New York Cook Book** are presented in a simple, easy-to-follow format so you can prepare authentic dishes in your home!

"Give me your tired, your poor, your huddled masses yearning to breathe free, the wretched refuse of your teeming shore. Send these, the homeless, tempest-tost, to me: I lift my lamp beside the golden door!"

from *The New Colossus* by
Emma Lazarus, 1883

New York Facts

Size – 30th largest state with an area of 47,214 square miles
Population – 18,976,457
State Capital – Albany
Statehood – July 26, 1788, the 11th state
    admitted to the Union
State Fruit – Apple
State Beverage – Milk
State Fish – Brook Trout
State Flower – Rose
State Nickname – The Empire State
State Song – "I Love New York"
State Motto – *Excelsior* (Ever Upward)

State Bird
Bluebird

State Tree
Sugar Maple

Famous New Yorkers

Kareem Abdul-Jabbar, basketball player; **Lucille Ball,** actress; **Humphrey Bogart,** actor; **James Cagney,** actor; **Maria Callas,** soprano; **Paddy Chayefsky,** playwright; **Aaron Copeland,** composer; **Tom Cruise,** actor; **Sammy Davis, Jr.,** actor/singer; **Agnes de Mille;** choreographer; **George Eastman,** inventor; **Henry Louis Gehrig,** baseball player; **Sarah Gellar,** actress; **George Gershwin,** composer; **Jackie Gleason,** comedian/actor; **Bret Harte,** writer; **Edward Hopper,** painter; **Washington Irving,** author; **Billy Joel,** singer/composer; **Michael J. Jordan,** basketball player; **Jerome Kern,** composer; **Rockwell Kent,** painter; **Vince Lombardi,** football coach; **Chico, Groucho, Harpo, Zeppo Marx,** comedians; **Herman Melville,** author; **Ethel Merman,** singer/actress; **Ogden Nash,** poet; **Rosie O'Donnell,** comedian; **Eugene O'Neill,** playwright; **George Pullman,** inventor; **Christopher Reeve,** actor; **John D. Rockefeller,** industrialist; **Norman Rockwell,** painter; **Mickey Rooney,** actor; **Jonas Salk,** polio researcher; **Barbara Stanwyck,** actress; **Rise Stevens,** mezzo-soprano; **Barbra Streisand,** singer/actress; **Tupac Shakur,** rapper; **Louis Comfort Tiffany,** painter/craftsman; **Mae West,** actress; **George Westinghouse Jr.,** inventor; **Walt Whitman,** poet; **Frank Winfield Woolworth,** merchant.

**U. S.
Presidents
from
New York**

Martin Van Buren   Millard Fillmore   Theodore Roosevelt   Franklin D. Roosevelt

New York Visitor Information: (800) 225-5697

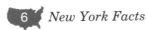

The Brooklyn Bridge

The Brooklyn Bridge, a suspension bridge over the East River, connects the boroughs of Brooklyn and Manhattan in New York City. When completed in 1883, it was the largest suspension bridge in the world. In 1964, the National Park Service designated the Brooklyn Bridge a national historic landmark.

Buffalo Wings

New York State Division of Tourism—Albany

24 CHICKEN WINGS
SALT and PEPPER
4 cups VEGETABLE or
 CORN OIL
1/4 cup BUTTER

2-5 Tbsp. HOT SAUCE
1 tsp. WHITE VINEGAR
CELERY STICKS
CARROT STICKS

Cut off tips and separate each wing at the joint. Season with salt and pepper to taste. Heat oil in a deep fryer or large heavy pot. When hot, add half of the wings. Cook about 10 minutes, stirring occasionally. When wings are golden brown and crisp, remove and drain well. Place in a large bowl. Add remaining wings to hot oil and repeat process. Meanwhile, melt butter in a saucepan. Add hot sauce to taste and then vinegar. Pour sauce over wings and mix well to cover. Serve with celery and carrot sticks, with *Blue Cheese Dressing* on the side.

Blue Cheese Dressing

1 cup MAYONNAISE
2 ONIONS, finely chopped
1 tsp. finely minced GARLIC
1/4 cup chopped PARSLEY
1/2 cup SOUR CREAM

1 Tbsp. LEMON JUICE
1/4 cup crumbled BLUE
 CHEESE
SALT and PEPPER

Combine all ingredients in a bowl, seasoning with salt and pepper to taste.

Buffalo

Buffalo, covering 50 square miles, is the second largest city in the state and one of the major industrial and transportation centers of the United States. It is the nation's largest producer of flour and one of its biggest grain-handling ports. Originally called New Amsterdam, Buffalo became the official name of this city in 1816. The city of Niagara Falls is Buffalo's largest suburb.

Catskills
Ham & Rye Balls

6 HARD-BOILED EGGS, chopped
1 Tbsp. minced CHIVES
1 cup minced cooked HAM

Pinch of PEPPER
3 Tbsp. RYE WHISKEY
1/2 cup ground WALNUTS

In a medium bowl, mix together all ingredients except nuts to a smooth consistency. Roll into 36 (1-inch) balls. Place nuts in a bowl and roll balls in nuts until well-coated. Insert toothpick in each and refrigerate.

New York City's Subway System

The official New York City subway system opened on October 27, 1904. Today, it serves 4.3 million customers on an average weekday and about 1.3 billion customers annually. There are 468 subway stations with 5,811 total trains that run an average of 1,000,000 miles per day.

Zesty Cheese Spread

"This spread is excellent on crackers and fresh vegetables."

Stephanie Melvin—The Westchester House, Saratoga Springs

2 cloves GARLIC, minced
2 pkgs. (8 oz. ea.) CREAM
   CHEESE, softened
1 cup BUTTER, softened
1/4 tsp. PEPPER
1/4 tsp. SALT

1/2 tsp. OREGANO
1/4 tsp. THYME
1/4 tsp. BASIL
1/4 tsp. MARJORAM
1/4 tsp. DILL

In a food processor, combine all ingredients until well-blended. Chill for 24 hours. Remove from refrigerator 30 minutes before serving.

Makes 3 cups.

Chopped Liver
(Gehakte Leber)

"Many serious eaters feel that chopped liver is the true test of a good Jewish cook. Prepare this recipe in a wooden bowl with an old-fashioned metal chopper, never in a food processor or blender. Chopping by hand gives the liver the right texture— coarse but not chunky."

The Kosher Gourmet Cookbook—New York City

1 lb. CHICKEN or STEER LIVERS
3-4 Tbsp. SCHMALTZ, divided
3 med. ONIONS, peeled and finely chopped
2 HARD-BOILED EGGS
1-2 Tbsp. chopped GRIBENES
SALT and freshly ground PEPPER

Broil livers thoroughly until no trace of pink remains. In a skillet, heat 1 tablespoon *Schmaltz* over medium-low heat. Add onions; sauté 5-10 minutes, until soft but not brown. In a wooden bowl with metal chopper, coarsely chop livers and eggs together. Add onions and drippings from skillet; chop a little longer until well-combined (do not form a paste.) Add 1-2 tablespoons chopped *Gribenes* and enough *Schmaltz* to moisten. Season to taste with salt and pepper.

Schmaltz & Gribenes

1/2 lb. CHICKEN FAT (from 2-3 chickens or 1 large fowl)
1/4 lb. CHICKEN SKIN, cut into small pieces

In a large heavy skillet, combine chicken fat and skin over medium-low heat. Cook slowly for 35-45 minutes, until fat liquefies and skin becomes golden and crisp. Strain liquid fat into a glass jar and store in refrigerator. Reserve gribenes (cracklings) to eat as a snack, toss into chopped liver mixture or use as a garnish for mashed potatoes or noodles.

> • **Schmaltz** (or **schmalz**) is fat rendered from chicken fat and skin. **Gribenes** is the cooked skin that remains after the rendering process.

New York City Knish

A knish (kuh NISH) is a baked Jewish pastry that may be filled with savory (potatoes, corned beef, ground beef, mushrooms) or sweet (nuts and raisins).

Dough:
- 2 cups FLOUR
- 1/2 tsp. BAKING POWDER
- 1/4 tsp. SALT
- 1/4 cup BUTTER or SCHMALTZ
- 1 EGG
- 2 Tbsp. WATER

Filling:
- 4 med. RUSSET POTATOES, peeled
- 2 Tbsp. BUTTER or SCHMALTZ
- 1/4 ONION, minced
- 1/2 tsp. SALT
- 1/8 tsp. GROUND BLACK PEPPER

In a bowl, sift flour, baking powder and salt. In another bowl, beat butter, egg and water. Combine mixtures and mix until smooth dough is formed. Set in a warm place for 45 minutes. While dough is setting, prepare filling. Halve or quarter potatoes, place in a saucepan and cover with water; boil until tender (15-20 minutes). Mash potatoes and place in a large bowl. In a skillet, add butter and sauté onion until translucent. Add onion, salt and pepper to mashed potatoes and stir well. Knead dough on a lightly floured surface, divide in half and roll out each half into 1/8-inch thick rectangles. Spread half of the filling on each rectangle and roll them up jelly roll style. Cut into 1-inch slices; pinch open ends closed and place on a well-greased baking sheet. Combine **1 beaten EGG** with **1/4 cup WATER** and brush over tops of each knish. Bake at 375° for 30 minutes or until golden brown.

America's Oldest Kosher Winery!
In 1899, Schapiro's began the kosher wine industry in New York City with their extra heavy original Concord Wine.

Empanada Appetizers

*"I have been cooking Spanish-style food since
I was a child in Puerto Rico."*

Margarita Barrett—Jackson Heights

2/3 cup VEGETABLE OIL	1 1/2 Tbsp. SALT
6 Tbsp. MARGARINE	8 cups FLOUR
1 1/2 cups WATER	1/2 cup DRY WHITE WINE
1/2 cup MILK	OIL for frying

Place oil and margarine in a small saucepan and heat until margarine has melted. Add water, milk and salt and bring to a boil over medium heat. In a large mixing bowl, combine flour, wine and margarine mixture. Stir gently. Cover and let rest for 1 hour. Roll dough out onto a lightly floured surface to 1/16-inch thickness. Cut into 2 or 3-inch circles. Add 1-2 tablespoons **Empanada Filling** to circles. Dampen edges with water and fold. Seal edges with tines of a fork, then prick tops with fork to vent. Heat 2-3 inches of oil in a deep skillet. Fry empanadas a few at a time until golden brown, turn and brown other side. Drain on paper towels.

Empanada Filling

3 med. ONIONS, chopped	3 cloves GARLIC, minced
3 Tbsp. MARGARINE	2 tsp. PEPPER
3 lbs. GROUND BEEF, CHICKEN	1 Tbsp. SALT
or TURKEY	2 Tbsp. PAPRIKA

In a skillet, sauté onions in margarine; add meat and cook until just brown. Drain off all drippings, add seasonings and combine.

The "Big Apple"—Version I

According to David Ellis' "Lonely Planet—New York City Guide," the city was named the Big Apple because a writer covering horse races in 1920 said in the "Morning Telegraph," that stable hands in New Orleans referred to a trip to a NY racecourse as going to the "Big Apple," or the greatest reward for any thoroughbred.

Pepperoni Rolls

*"I combined two of my favorite cuisines for
this tasty appetizer."*

Andrew Puma—Ronkonkoma

1/2 lb. PEPPERONI, cut into 16 slices
1 lb. MOZZARELLA CHEESE, cut into 16 slices
8 EGG ROLL WRAPPERS
OLIVE OIL for frying

Place 2 slices of pepperoni and 2 slices of cheese in the center of each wrapper. Roll according to package directions. Fry until brown on all sides. Drain and let cool slightly before serving.

Salami Pie Slices

6 oz. MUENSTER CHEESE,
  shredded
1 EGG, beaten
3/4 cup FLOUR
1/2 tsp. SALT
1/8 tsp. PEPPER
1 cup MILK
1/4 cup chopped SALAMI
1/2 tsp. OREGANO

Reserve 2-3 tablespoons of cheese. In a bowl, combine all ingredients. Pour into a well-greased 8-inch pie plate. Bake for 30 minutes in a 425° oven. Top with reserved cheese. Bake for 2 more minutes or until cheese melts. Let cool for 5 minutes and then slice into small wedges.

♪ ## New York Song Sampler

I'll Take Manhattan ● *Sunday in New York* ● *Take the A Train* ● *Mona Lisas and Mad Hatters* ● *New York State of Mind* ● *New York, New York* ● *Sidewalks of New York* ● *Give My Regards to Broadway* ● *The Fifty-Ninth Street Bridge Song* ● *Stayin' Alive* ● *On Broadway* ● *Autumn in New York* ● *I Love New York* ● *The Erie Canal* ● *Buffalo Gals.*

Baba Ghanoush

A Middle Eastern dish (bah-bah-gha-NOOSH).

1 med. EGGPLANT
1/4 cup TAHINI
1 Tbsp. LEMON JUICE
1 clove GARLIC
1/4 tsp. BLACK PEPPER
Dash of GROUND CUMIN
2 Tbsp. SESAME SEEDS
2 Tbsp. finely chopped FRESH PARSLEY

Peel egplant and cut into 1/2-inch cubes (about 3 cups); steam until tender, about 8 minutes. Place eggplant in food processor, add tahini, lemon juice and garlic. Purée. Stir in remaining ingredients, except parsley. Spoon mixture into a serving bowl and garnish with parsley. Serve warm or chilled.

> **Did You Know?**
> *Due to its increasing popularity, the production of eggplant on farms in New York has more than doubled in the last decade!*

Clam Delight

"This is always the first to go when I serve it at a party."

Victoria Staskiel—Centereach

2 cans (6 oz. ea.) MINCED CLAMS
1 cup ITALIAN SEASONED
   BREAD CRUMBS
1 stick MARGARINE
1/2 cup chopped ONION

1 tsp. LEMON JUICE
1 tsp. OREGANO
Dash of GARLIC POWDER
Dash of PEPPER

Drain clams and spread evenly in a pie plate. Sprinkle with bread crumbs. In a medium skillet, sauté remaining ingredients in margarine until onions are tender. Spoon onion mixture over bread crumbs in pie plate. Bake at 350° for 20-25 minutes or until browned. Let set and then cut into wedges.

Savory Pork Meatballs with Curry Sauce

New York Pork Producers—Bergen

1 lb. GROUND PORK
1/2 cup SOFT BREAD CRUMBS
1 EGG, beaten
2 Tbsp. minced ONION
1 Tbsp. minced GREEN BELL PEPPER
1 clove GARLIC, minced
1 tsp. SALT
1/8 tsp. PEPPER
1 Tbsp. VEGETABLE OIL

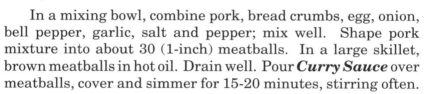

In a mixing bowl, combine pork, bread crumbs, egg, onion, bell pepper, garlic, salt and pepper; mix well. Shape pork mixture into about 30 (1-inch) meatballs. In a large skillet, brown meatballs in hot oil. Drain well. Pour *Curry Sauce* over meatballs, cover and simmer for 15-20 minutes, stirring often.

Curry Sauce

1 can (8 oz.) TOMATO SAUCE
1/4 cup APPLE JELLY
1/4 tsp. CURRY POWDER

In a small saucepan, combine all ingredients. Simmer until jelly is melted, stirring occasionally.

The "Big Apple"—Version II

Rumor has it that the "Big Apple" is so named because during the depression, many former financiers would travel from their suburban cottages in order to sell apples on the streets of New York City. Several well-to-do families had to make ends meet by selling apples and the charade became known to many as the "Big Apple" scam of New York.

Veal Meatballs in Sweet & Sour Sauce

Maria Battaglia—La Cucina Italiana, Inc., New York City

1 lb. GROUND VEAL
1 lg. EGG
1/2 cup PARMESAN CHEESE
1/2 cup DRY BREAD CRUMBS

1/4 cup chopped ITALIAN
   FLAT-LEAF PARSLEY
1/4 cup chopped fresh BASIL
SALT and PEPPER

Combine all ingredients and mix thoroughly, seasoning with salt and pepper to taste. Shape into 1-inch balls. Place on a baking sheet. Bake at 400° for 15-20 minutes until browned and temperature of meatballs reaches 160°. Drain on paper towels and allow to cool while preparing *Sweet & Sour Sauce.*

Sweet & Sour Sauce

1/2 cup diced ONION
3 Tbsp. OLIVE OIL
2 cups chopped canned
   PLUM TOMATOES
1 tsp. SALT

5 Tbsp. SUGAR
3 Tbsp. RED WINE VINEGAR
3 Tbsp. chopped ITALIAN
   FLAT-LEAF PARSLEY

Sauté onion in oil until translucent. Add tomatoes and salt. Simmer for 5 minutes over low heat. Stir in sugar and vinegar. Add meatballs and simmer until heated through, about 6-10 minutes. Before serving, garnish with parsley.

Artichoke Dip

Karen Hallenbeck—Clifton Park

1 cup MAYONNAISE
1/2 lb. SWISS CHEESE, shredded
1 can (14 oz.) unmarinated ARTICHOKE
   HEARTS, cut up

In a bowl, combine all ingredients together. Pour into a baking dish and bake at 350° until edges start to brown, about 15-20 minutes. Serve with crackers.

Long Island

Long Island extends 125 miles east of Manhattan. In Nassau County, the north side of the island is known as the "Gold Coast" and contains beautiful gardens and elegant estates. Suffolk County boasts some of the most productive farmland in the entire state. The island is home to commercial fishermen, and its beaches, docks and jetties provide excellent recreational opportunities. Jones Beach and Fire Island National Seashore are two of the many popular beaches that can be found on the shores of this island. Here, too, you will find the Hamptons, where many summer vacationers stay and play.

The Six Sisters Vegetable Quiche

The Six Sisters Bed & Breakfast—Saratoga Springs

1 (9-inch) unbaked PIE SHELL
3/4 cup MILK
3/4 cup HALF AND HALF
2 Tbsp. melted BUTTER
4 EGGS
Dash of NUTMEG
Dash of CAYENNE
1 Tbsp. FLOUR

1 Tbsp. diced ONION
1 cup diced BROCCOLI
1 1/2 cups sliced MUSHROOMS
3/4 cup shredded CHEDDAR
   CHEESE
3/4 cup shredded MONTEREY
   JACK CHEESE WITH
   JALAPEÑO

In a 375° oven, bake pie shell for 5 minutes. In a mixing bowl, combine milk, half and half, butter, eggs, nutmeg, cayenne and flour; set aside. Sprinkle onion on bottom of pie shell. Layer with broccoli, mushrooms and cheeses. Pour egg mixture on top. Bake for 40 minutes. Let cool 10 minutes before serving.

Garden Brunch Sandwiches

"I tasted a similar recipe at a garden brunch, then developed this one to suit my own tastes."

Lynda Lumley-Katzman—Sayville

4 lg. slices HERB BREAD
4-6 oz. PESTO SAUCE
4 oz. MOZZARELLA CHEESE, sliced
1-2 lg. BEEFSTEAK TOMATOES, sliced
2 oil-packed ROASTED RED PEPPERS, halved
2 oz. oil-packed SUN-DRIED TOMATOES, chopped
BALSAMIC VINEGAR

Place bread on a baking sheet and spread each slice with pesto sauce. Top with cheese, tomatoes and red pepper. Sprinkle with sun-dried tomatoes. Broil for 2-3 minutes on lower rack or until heated through. Drizzle with balsamic vinegar and serve.

Baked Omelet

"This is a great recipe for weekend breakfasts and brunches, paired with fresh fruit and sweet rolls. Add bacon, mushrooms, chives and peppers for variety."

Carolyn Rudolph— Sanford's Ridge Bed & Breakfast, Queensbury

8 slices WHITE BREAD, cut into
   1-inch cubes
1 Tbsp. BUTTER
1/2 lb. EXTRA SHARP CHEDDAR
   CHEESE, grated
1 tsp. DRY MUSTARD
8 EGGS
3 cups LOW FAT MILK
1 tsp. SALT
Dash of CAYENNE

Layer bread cubes on bottom of a greased 13 x 9 glass baking dish. Dot with butter and sprinkle with cheese and mustard. Set aside. In a large bowl, beat together eggs, milk, salt and cayenne. Pour mixture over bread cubes. Refrigerate for 6 hours or overnight. Cover and bake in a 350° oven for about 1 hour, uncovering to brown during the last 15 minutes.

Italian Baked Frittata

Carolyn Farnsworth—Towering Maples Bed & Breakfast, Durhamville

1 cup BROCCOLI FLORETS
1/2 cup sliced MUSHROOMS
1/2 RED BELL PEPPER, cut
   into rings
2 bunches GREEN ONIONS,
   sliced into 1-inch pieces
1 Tbsp. MARGARINE
8 EGGS
1/4 cup GREY POUPON® MUSTARD
1/4 cup WATER
1/2 tsp. ITALIAN SEASONING
1 cup shredded SWISS CHEESE

In a skillet, sauté broccoli, mushrooms, bell pepper and green onions in margarine for 5 minutes or until tender. Place vegetable mixture in a casserole dish. In a bowl, use mixer to combine eggs, mustard, water and Italian seasoning until foamy. Stir in cheese. Pour over vegetables. Bake in a 375° oven for 20-25 minutes or until set.

Apple Lasagna

8 LASAGNA NOODLES	6 Tbsp. FLOUR
2 cans (21 oz. ea.) APPLE PIE FILLING	6 Tbsp. BROWN SUGAR
2 cups shredded CHEDDAR CHEESE	1/4 cup QUICK OATS
1 cup RICOTTA CHEESE	1/2 tsp. CINNAMON
1 EGG	Dash of NUTMEG
1/4 cup SUGAR	3 Tbsp. BUTTER,
1 tsp. ALMOND EXTRACT	chunked

Cook lasagna noodles according to package directions. Grease an 11 x 9 casserole dish. Spread 1 can of apple filling on bottom. Lay 4 noodles over apple filling. In a small bowl, combine cheeses, egg, sugar and almond extract. Pour over noodles. Top with remaining noodles. Spread second can of apple filling on top. In a bowl, combine remaining ingredients. Spread over apple filling. Bake 45 minutes in a 350° oven. Cool 15 minutes before serving.

No-Bake Tofu Quiche

"This quick and easy quiche contains no dairy products."

Ali Dorian—*New York New Wave Health Recipes*, Staten Island

1 lb. FIRM TOFU, rinsed and drained
1 pkg. (10 oz.) FIRM SILKEN TOFU
1 Tbsp. TAMARI (SOY SAUCE)
1/2 tsp. SEA SALT
4 Tbsp. CASHEW NUT BUTTER
1 clove GARLIC, minced
2 oz. fresh PARSLEY, minced
2 Tbsp. WHOLE-WHEAT BREAD CRUMBS
2 med. ZUCCHINI, sliced
4 oz. MUSHROOMS, sliced

Combine first 8 ingredients in a food processor or blender and process until well-blended. Arrange zucchini in an 8-inch pie plate and top with mushrooms. Spoon tofu mixture over vegetables. Chill until firm.

Stuffed French Toast

"You're sure to win rave reviews with this recipe!"

Diane Van Der Woude—Sutherland House–A Bed & Breakfast Inn, Canandaigua

20 slices CINNAMON SWIRL
    BREAD
6 EGGS
4 cups HALF AND HALF

2 tsp. VANILLA
1 cup SUGAR

Filling:
    2 pkgs. (8 oz. ea.) CREAM
        CHEESE, softened
    1 tsp. VANILLA
    2 EGGS
    1/2 cup SUGAR

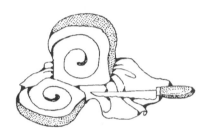

Dash of NUTMEG
SYRUP
POWDERED SUGAR

Spray a 15 x 11 baking pan and a single loaf pan with cooking spray. Arrange 8 pieces of bread in 15 x 11 pan, 2 pieces in loaf pan so that the bottoms are covered. In a bowl, mix eggs, half and half, vanilla and sugar. Pour half of egg mixture over bread. In another bowl, cream filling ingredients until smooth. Pour over moistened bread. Arrange remaining bread over top of filling and pour remaining egg mixture over top. Sprinkle with nutmeg. Cover with plastic wrap and let stand in refrigerator overnight. Preheat oven to 350°. Uncover and bake for 60 minutes. Let stand 10 minutes before cutting. To serve: Cut each serving diagonally and open it up slightly to reveal the filling. Drizzle with syrup and sprinkle with powdered sugar.

Canandaigua

This city is situated on the shores of 17-mile long Canandaigua Lake, one of the beautiful Finger Lakes of western New York.

Banana Pecan Pancakes

"Our Inn is listed on the National Register of Historic Places and was featured in the world renowned series of books 'America's Painted Ladies.'"

Kim Molisani—The Painted Lady Bed & Breakfast, Elmira

1 cup FLOUR	2 Tbsp. melted BUTTER
1/2 cup WHOLE-WHEAT FLOUR	2 tsp. HONEY
1/4 cup CORNMEAL	2 Tbsp. BUTTER
1/4 cup chopped toasted PECANS	2 BANANAS, sliced
1/2 tsp. BAKING SODA	1/4 cup toasted PECAN
1 EGG	HALVES
1 1/2 cups BUTTERMILK	WHIPPED CREAM
1/3 cup mashed ripe BANANA	

In a large bowl, combine flours, cornmeal, chopped pecans and baking soda; set aside. In another bowl, mix egg, buttermilk, mashed banana, melted butter and honey; stir into flour mixture until just moistened. Heat griddle and grease with cooking spray, oil or shortening. Pour batter by 1/4 cupfuls onto hot griddle. Cook about 2 minutes or until pancakes are puffed and dry at outer edges. Turn and cook other sides until golden brown. Melt butter in a skillet over medium heat. Sauté sliced bananas, stirring occasionally, until they have softened and are golden brown. When serving, top pancakes with ***Orange Topping,*** sautéed bananas, pecan halves and dollops of whipped cream.

Orange Topping

1/4 cup packed DARK BROWN SUGAR
1/4 cup ORANGE JUICE
2 Tbsp. BUTTER

Combine all ingredients in a 2-quart saucepan. Cook over medium heat for about 5 minutes, stirring occasionally, until mixture boils and thickens. Keep warm until ready to serve.

Brooklyn Egg Cream

Despite its name, the egg cream contains no eggs or cream! What you need are the basic ingredients, and a New York attitude!

1 cup MILK
SPARKLING SELTZER WATER
2 Tbsp. FOX'S U-BET® CHOCOLATE SYRUP

Pour milk into a tall glass, add seltzer water until a white head reaches the top of the glass. Spoon in syrup with a little wrist action and enjoy this New York favorite!

New York Cocktail

Juice of 1 LIME
1 tsp. POWDERED SUGAR
1 1/2 oz. BLENDED SCOTCH WHISKY
1/2 tsp. GRANADINE
ICE

Shake all ingredients together with ice and then strain into a cocktail glass. Garnish with a twist of lemon peel.

New York Lemonade

2 oz. LEMON JUICE   1 oz. CLUB SODA
2 oz. LEMON VODKA   LEMON
1 oz. GRAND MARNIER   SUGAR

Blend lemon juice, vodka, Grand Marnier and club soda. Strain into chilled cocktail glasses. Rub edge of glasses with sliced lemon and sugar the rim.

New York City—Capital of the United States!
New York City served as the capital of the United States from 1785 to 1790. George Washington took the oath of office as the nation's first President in New York City on April 30, 1789.

New York Sour

2 oz. BLENDED SCOTCH WHISKY   CLARET
JUICE of 1/2 LEMON   1/2 SLICE LEMON
1 tsp. POWDERED SUGAR   MARASCHINO CHERRY
ICE

Shake whisky, lemon juice and powdered sugar with ice and strain into a sour glass. Float claret (to taste) on top. Garnish with lemon and cherry.

Long Island Iced Tea

1/2 oz. RUM   1 oz. LEMONADE
1/2 oz. GIN   COCA COLA®
1/2 oz. VODKA   7-UP®
1/2 oz. TRIPLE SEC

Pour first 5 ingredients over ice in a tall glass. Add equal amounts of Coca Cola and 7-Up. Garnish with a **LEMON WEDGE.**

Ring in the New Year!

Since 1907, the tradition of the Ball Lowering in Times Square has become a universal symbol of welcoming the New Year!

The Original Manhattan

1/4-1/2 oz. SWEET VERMOUTH
1 1/2 oz. CANADIAN WHISKY
Dash ANGOSTURA BITTERS

Adjusting vermouth to taste, combine all ingredients with ice in a pitcher or shaker. Strain into a chilled cocktail glass.

SOUPS & SALADS

New York's Empire State Building

The Empire State Building, located on 34th Street between Fifth Avenue and the Avenue of the Americas, is one of the world's tallest office buildings. Soaring 1,472 feet, the building has 2 million square feet of office space. Visitors can see approximately 50 miles from the 86th floor observatory. Another observation tower, the circular glass-enclosed tower on the 102nd floor, offers more views for the not-so-faint of heart.

Manhattan Clam Chowder

3 cups (about 24) fresh CLAMS or canned minced CLAMS
2 cups CLAM JUICE or WATER
1/2 cup finely diced SALT PORK
1/2 cup chopped ONION
1/2 cup sliced CELERY
2 cups diced POTATOES
3 cups chopped TOMATOES
1/4 tsp. THYME
SALT and PEPPER
2 Tbsp. chopped fresh PARSLEY
6 PILOT BISCUITS or SODA CRACKERS

If using fresh clams, steam them in water using a heavy iron pot. When cooked, remove from pot reserving the liquid. Shell and mince clams. If using canned clams, drain clam liquid and reserve. Add enough water to reserved liquid to equal 2 cups; set aside. In a skillet, sauté salt pork until brown. Add onion and sauté until tender. Place salt pork mixture in a large saucepan. Add celery, potatoes and clam liquid. Simmer over medium heat until potatoes are done. Add tomatoes and thyme and season with salt and pepper to taste; add clams. Simmer for an additional 10 minutes. Add parsley. To serve, place biscuits on bottom of soup bowls and add chowder.

Serves 4-6.

The Statue of Liberty

The Statue of Liberty has been a beacon of freedom for arriving immigrants for over 100 years. The statue, presented to the United States by the French as a symbol of friendship and democracy, was dedicated on October 28th, 1886. Liberty stands 151 feet tall and weighs 450,000 pounds. For her hundredth birthday, the statue was treated to handsome renovations by a team of French and American craftsmen. Today it boasts a new glass-walled elevator, extensive museum exhibits and a handcrafted torch complete with gold-plated flame.

Hearty Veal Stew

New York Veal Growers—Westmoreland

4 tsp. OLIVE OIL
2 lbs. VEAL, cut into 1 1/2-inch pieces
2 cups WATER, divided
1 med. ONION, coarsely chopped
1/2 cup DRY WHITE WINE
2 tsp. ITALIAN SEASONING
3/4 tsp. SALT
1 1/2 cups medium-sized PASTA SHELLS
1 1/2 cups chopped GREEN, RED or YELLOW BELL
    PEPPER, or a combination
1 Tbsp. CORNSTARCH
1/2 cup pitted RIPE OLIVES, drained
1 Tbsp. BALSAMIC VINEGAR

In a Dutch oven or deep skillet, heat oil over medium heat. Add veal and brown evenly, stirring occasionally. Pour off drippings. Add 1 3/4 cups water, onion, wine and seasonings. Cover tightly and simmer for 1 hour or until veal is tender. Cook pasta according to package directions; drain and set aside. Add bell pepper to veal mixture. Bring stew to a boil over medium-high heat. In a bowl, dissolve cornstarch in 1/4 cup water and add to stew. Cook and stir for 2 minutes or until sauce is thickened and bubbly. Add pasta, olives and vinegar to stew; heat through.

Chilled Tomato Soup

Stephanie Melvin—The Westchester House Bed & Breakfast Inn,
Saratoga Springs

2 cans (16 oz. ea.) TOMATOES, undrained
4 GREEN ONIONS, minced
1 tsp. SUGAR
1 Tbsp. chopped fresh PARSLEY
1/4 tsp. BASIL
2 cups PLAIN YOGURT

In a food processor or blender, purée tomatoes. Add remaining ingredients and blend well. Chill for 3-4 hours.

Hudson Valley Cheese Soup

"This is a favorite of the Hudson Valley Dutch."

New York Division of Tourism—Albany

1 Tbsp. finely minced ONION
2 Tbsp. BUTTER
2 Tbsp. FLOUR
2 cups well-seasoned CHICKEN STOCK
1/2 cup cooked and mashed CARROTS
2 cups HALF AND HALF
1 cup grated SHARP CHEDDAR
    CHEESE
Chopped PARSLEY

Sauté onion in butter until just translucent. Blend in flour. Add stock, carrots and half and half. Cook, stirring constantly, until slightly thickened. Add cheese and continue stirring until cheese is thoroughly melted. Serve very hot, garnished generously with parsley.

Oyster Stew

24 sm. shucked OYSTERS
2 Tbsp. BUTTER
Dash of WORCESTERSHIRE SAUCE
2 cups MILK
2 cups LIGHT CREAM
SALT and PEPPER
CELERY SALT
CRACKERS

Drain oysters, reserving liquid. In a saucepan, combine oysters, 2 tablespoons oysters liquid, butter and Worcestershire sauce. Cook over low heat until edges of oysters begin to curl. Remove oysters and set aside. Add remaining oyster liquid and bring to a boil. In another saucepan, heat milk and cream until bubbles form around edges of pan. Combine oysters, liquid and milk mixtures. Season with salt, pepper and celery salt to taste. Serve with crackers.

Matzo Ball Soup

It is said that this soup's curative powers are released only when the vegetables are mashed together in the soup bowl!

Chicken Soup

(New York Penicillin)

1 (3-5 lb.) CHICKEN, whole or parts	2 stalks CELERY
4 qts. COLD WATER	1 bunch fresh PARSLEY
2 CARROTS, halved lengthwise	1 lg. ONION, halved
1 PARSNIP	SALT and PEPPER

Quarter chicken, place in a large pot and cover with cold water. Tie carrots, parsnip, celery and parsley together with thread. Place vegetables in pot with chicken, along with onion, salt and pepper. Bring to a boil, reduce heat and simmer for 3 hours, skimming frequently. Remove chicken; skin, debone, and set chicken aside for other recipes. Remove bundled vegetables and onion, discarding parsnip, parsley and onion. Slice carrots and celery and return to pot. Cover pot and keep warm over low heat until ready to serve.

Matzo Balls

6 EGGS	1/2 tsp. NUTMEG
3 heaping Tbsp. SCHMALTZ	2 Tbsp. chopped
(see p. 10) or 1/3 cup OIL	PARSLEY
1 1/2 cups MATZO MEAL	WATER
1 tsp. SALT	1 Tbsp. SALT

Beat eggs until fluffy; stir in schmaltz. Gradually fold in matzo meal, salt, nutmeg and parsley. Cover and refrigerate at least 1/2 hour. Bring a large pot of salted water to a boil. Run hands under cold water (so matzo mixture won't stick to your hands) and scoop out enough mixture to form into a 1 1/2-inch ball. Put each ball directly in the boiling water, as you make it. They will rise to the top as they are done. Repeat process until all matzo balls are made. Cover pot and cook for 30-40 minutes. *Do not remove cover while cooking!* To serve: Place 2-3 matzo balls in each soup bowl; ladle chicken broth, carrots and celery over top.

Classic Caesar Salad

Michael W. Terrio—Terrio's Carriage House, Schroon Lake

**6 cups MIXED SALAD GREENS, washed, dried and
broken into bite-size pieces
1 cup 1/2-inch CROUTONS (preferably from sourdough bread)
2 Tbsp. GARLIC OIL*
JUICE of 1 1/2 LEMONS
1 1/2 tsp. WORCESTERSHIRE SAUCE
6 Tbsp. FRENCH DRESSING
1 (1-minute) CODDLED EGG
1 tsp. freshly ground BLACK PEPPER
4 Tbsp. grated PARMESAN CHEESE**

Prepare salad greens, croutons and garlic oil. At serving time, beat together garlic oil, lemon juice, Worcestershire sauce, French dressing and egg. In a large wooden bowl, toss salad greens, croutons, egg mixture, pepper and Parmesan cheese. Serve immediately.

*To prepare garlic oil: Place 1 peeled garlic clove in 2 tablespoons oil and let stand several hours; remove garlic.

Spicy Carrot-Bean Salad

Edna Gardner—Schenectady

**4 med. CARROTS
1/2 lb. fresh GREEN BEANS
1/2 cup CIDER VINEGAR
1 cup WATER
1/2 tsp. SALT**

**1 tsp. minced ONION
1 tsp. MUSTARD SEEDS
1 clove GARLIC, minced
1 Tbsp. DILL WEED**

Peel and trim carrots and place in a saucepan. Add enough water to cover and bring to a boil. Cook for 3 minutes, then remove from heat and drain. Cool and cut into 4-inch strips. Wash and trim beans, leaving whole. In a saucepan, combine vinegar, water, salt, onion, mustard seeds, garlic and dill weed. Bring to a boil. Add carrots and beans. Reduce heat and simmer for 5 minutes. Remove from heat and cool. Place in a glass or ceramic dish, cover and chill for 1-2 days. Serve cold.

Grilled Vegetable Salad

Chef John DeSantis, Sous-Chef Dan Aziz—Bavarian Chalet,
Guilderland

1 ZUCCHINI
2 YELLOW SQUASH
1 lg. ONION
1 EGGPLANT
OLIVE OIL
1 roasted RED CHILE
    PEPPER, diced
COARSE SALT
RED PEPPER FLAKES

Freshly ground BLACK
    PEPPER
Chopped fresh PARSLEY
OREGANO
1 clove GARLIC, minced
2 tsp. BALSAMIC VINEGAR
2 Tbsp. EXTRA VIRGIN
    OLIVE OIL

Slice zucchini and squash lengthwise into 1/4-inch thick
slices. Peel and slice onion into 1/4-inch thick rounds. Peel and
slice eggplant lengthwise into 1/2-inch thick slices. Rub all with
oil to coat. Grill until just soft, about 4 minutes per side.
Remove vegetables from grill, dice and place in a salad bowl. In
a bowl, combine remaining seasonings to taste with garlic,
vinegar and oil. Toss dressing with vegetables. Let sit at least
20 minutes to blend flavors. Serve at room temperature.

Did You Know?
*More than 40 different types of vegetables are commercially
grown in New York!*

Ed's Poppy Seed Dressing

Edward Gralow—Schenectady

2 tsp. CORNSTARCH
1/2 cup SUGAR
1/2 tsp. SALT
2/3 tsp. WATER
1/2 cup + 2 Tbsp. SALAD OIL

1/2 cup + 2 tsp. CIDER VINEGAR
1 tsp. MUSTARD
1 tsp. (heaping) DRY MUSTARD
1 tsp. (heaping) POPPY SEEDS

In a saucepan, combine all ingredients except mustards and
poppy seeds. Bring to a boil to thicken. Add mustards and
poppy seeds. Cool. Keep refrigerated until ready to serve.

Basset Café Chicken Salad

"Named after the owner's basset hound, Lucy, the Basset Café is an ideal hangout. This is one of the most popular dishes."

Martin Cowart—Basset Café, New York City

8 cooked boneless CHICKEN BREASTS, cut into 1-inch cubes
1 cup chopped CELERY
1 1/2 cups SEEDLESS GRAPES, cut in half
1/2 cup roasted PECAN PIECES
1/2 cup MAYONNAISE
1/3 cup SOUR CREAM or CRÈME FRAÎCHE
1 Tbsp. chopped fresh TARRAGON
SALT and PEPPER

In a bowl, combine all ingredients, seasoning with salt and pepper to taste; mix well. Cover and refrigerate. Served chilled.

Wild Mushroom Salad

Steve Stofelano, Jr.—Mansion Hill Inn, Albany

2 cups sliced WILD MUSHROOMS (shiitake, oyster or crimini)
1 1/2 cups sliced BUTTON MUSHROOMS
1/4 cup SUN-DRIED TOMATOES, rehydrated in hot water,
    drained and julienned
1/4 cup chopped roasted RED CHILE PEPPER
1/2 cup thinly sliced RED ONION
1 Tbsp. minced GARLIC
2 Tbsp. chopped fresh BASIL
2 tsp. OREGANO
1/4 cup BALSAMIC VINEGAR
1/2-3/4 cup OLIVE OIL
SALT and PEPPER
6 cups torn MIXED SALAD GREENS
Fresh BASIL LEAVES

In a 3-quart saucepan, combine all ingredients except salad greens and basil leaves. Let stand 1-2 hours at room temperature, stirring occasionally. When ready to serve, reheat. Divide greens among salad plates and spoon mushroom mixture over top. Garnish with basil leaves.

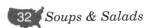

MAIN DISHES

New York City

New York City covers about 365 square miles, including 65 square miles of inland water. New York is the largest city in the United States in population and the seventh largest in the world. George Washington took the oath of office as the nation's first President in New York City on April 30, 1789. New York City served as the capital of the United States from 1785 to 1790. The city is divided into five areas called boroughs—The Bronx, Manhattan, Queens, Brooklyn, and Staten Island.

Asiago Cheese & Sun-Dried Tomato Steaks

Tara Fanuko—Bronx

1/4 cup FLOUR
SALT and PEPPER
8 (3 oz. ea.) BEEF TENDERLOIN
   FILET MIGNON STEAKS,
   about 1/2-inch thick
1 jar (8 oz.) oil-packed
   SUN-DRIED TOMATOES

3 GREEN ONIONS, chopped
4 lg. cloves GARLIC, minced
1 Tbsp. BASIL
1/2 cup grated ASIAGO
   CHEESE
CHERRY TOMATOES, sliced
BASIL LEAVES

Place flour on a plate and season with salt and pepper to taste. Lightly coat steaks with flour mixture and set aside. Drain sun-dried tomatoes, reserving oil. Pat tomatoes dry with a paper towel and finely chop; set aside. Heat a large skillet on high heat. Coat skillet well with one full tablespoon of reserved tomato oil. Reduce heat to medium and cook steaks four at a time for 2 1/2-3 minutes per side. Remove steaks and keep warm. Coat skillet with remaining tomato oil and add sun-dried tomatoes, onions and garlic. Stir-fry for 1-2 minutes. Stir in basil and cheese, continuing to stir until well mixed and cheese has melted. Remove from heat. Transfer meat to a serving platter and top each with two table-spoons of tomato mixture, pressing down with back of spoon. Garnish with cherry tomatoes and basil leaves.

Serves 4.

The Bronx

The Bronx is chiefly a residential borough with a population of over one million people. The eastern section is a broad plain, the western part consists of a series of hills and valleys. Fordham University and the New York University Hall of Fame, the New York Botanical Garden, world renowned Bronx Zoo and Yankee Stadium are all located here.

Long Island Seafood Lasagna

Beula Maris—Plainview

1 Tbsp. BUTTER
1 Tbsp. finely chopped SHALLOTS
3/4 lb. uncooked SHRIMP, peeled and deveined
1 pint SCALLOPS
SALT
Freshly ground PEPPER
1/2 cup WHITE WINE
2 cups thinly sliced MUSHROOMS
2 cups BÉCHAMEL SAUCE (see next page)
1 cup canned CRUSHED TOMATOES
1/2 cup HEAVY CREAM
1/4 tsp. crushed HOT RED PEPPER FLAKES or TABASCO®
3 Tbsp. finely chopped fresh PARSLEY
9 LASAGNA NOODLES
4 (1/4 lb.) boneless FLOUNDER FILLETS
1 cup grated GRUYÈRE or SWISS CHEESE

Melt butter in a large skillet and sauté shallots about 30 seconds; add shrimp and scallops. Season with salt and pepper to taste. When shrimp starts to turn pink, add wine. Cook until wine comes to a boil. Turn off heat. Using a slotted spoon, transfer seafood to a bowl. Bring the cooking liquid to a simmer and add mushrooms. Cook about 5 minutes. Stir in *Béchamel Sauce.* Add tomatoes and simmer for 5 minutes. Add cream, pepper flakes, parsley and any liquid which may have accumulated around reserved shrimp and scallops. Season with salt and pepper to taste. Preheat oven to 375°. Cook lasagna noodles according to package directions. Butter the bottom and sides of a 13 x 9 baking dish. Spoon a layer of sauce over the bottom. Add 1/2 of shrimp and scallop mixture. Spoon a layer of sauce over shrimp and scallops. Cover with three lasagna noodles. Add a layer of flounder, salt and pepper and a thin layer of sauce. Cover with three lasagna noodles. Scatter

(continued on next page)

Long Island Seafood Lasagna *(continued from previous page)*
remaining shrimp and scallops over the top and spoon a layer
of sauce over all, reserving enough sauce for a final layer. Cover
with remaining lasagna noodles. Spoon remaining sauce over
top. Sprinkle with cheese. Bake for 30 minutes.

Serves 8-10.

Béchamel Sauce

4 Tbsp. BUTTER
4 Tbsp. FLOUR
2 cups MILK

SALT
Freshly ground PEPPER

Melt butter in a saucepan, add flour, stirring with a wire
whisk. When blended, add milk whisking rapidly. Add salt and
pepper to taste. When thickened and smooth, reduce heat and
cook (stirring about every 5 minutes) for 20 minutes.

Spicy Mac & Jack

Heluva Good Cheese, Inc.—Sodus

2 qts. WATER
1 tsp. SALT
8 oz. ELBOW MACARONI
2 Tbsp. BUTTER or MARGARINE
1/4 cup chopped ONION
1/4 cup chopped RED BELL PEPPER
1 can (10.75 oz.) 98% FAT FREE CREAM OF CHICKEN SOUP
1 ctn. (16 oz.) HELUVA GOOD® FAT FREE SOUR CREAM
1/4 cup MILK
2 cups grated HELUVA GOOD® MONTEREY JACK with JALAPEÑO
1/2 cup crushed TORTILLA CHIPS

In a large saucepan, combine water and salt. Bring to a boil
and add macaroni. Stir and cook 8-10 minutes until al dente.
Drain. Rinse with cold water and drain again. In a saucepan,
melt butter over medium heat and sauté onion and bell pepper
until soft, about 3 minutes. Remove from heat. Stir in soup,
sour cream and milk. Add pasta and cheese. Toss gently to
evenly coat. Spoon into a greased 2-quart baking dish. Sprinkle
top with tortilla chips. Bake at 350° for 30-35 minutes.

Serves 6.

Vegan Sauté

"This dish is on our Specials menu and is very popular with our vegan customers. The Chef alters the ingredients weekly depending on what is in season and, therefore, most nourishing and flavorful. Spinach is a good green to use in place of the romaine or Swiss chard. You can use any kind of bean you have a taste for. I particularly like the chickpeas in this dish."

Kathy Kirkpatrick—Life Café, New York City

1/2 square ORGANIC TOFU, cubed or 1/2 cup sliced SEITAN
1 cup sliced ZUCCHINI
1 cup chopped MUSHROOMS
1 ONION, chopped
1/3 cup CHICKPEAS
1/3 cup chopped ROMAINE or RED SWISS CHARD LETTUCE
OIL
1 tsp. MARGARINE
SALT and PEPPER
Cooked LONG-GRAIN BROWN RICE, UDON or SOBA NOODLES

Steam together tofu and zucchini. Sauté mushrooms, onion, chickpeas and romaine in a little oil until cooked (if using seitan, add to this sauté). Add tofu and zucchini to sauté pan. Add **Miso Broth** and reduce. Add margarine; season with salt and pepper to taste. Serve over rice or noodles.

Serves 2.

Miso Broth

1/2 cup WATER   1 tsp. chopped fresh
1/2 Tbsp. MISO   GINGER

Blend ingredients together in a small bowl.

Did You Know?

Fruits and vegetables are New York's second most important farm products (after dairy). This state is a leader in growing onions, cabbage, apples, cherries, grapes, peaches, pears and strawberries. Nationally, New York is second to California in grape production and second to Washington in apple production.

Chicken in a Portobello Mushroom Cream Sauce

"Although this is a chicken dish, the use of balsamic vinegar and portobello mushrooms gives it a full, hard flavor, so a dry red wine goes well with it."

Chef Joseph Miranda—The Wheat Fields, Saratoga Springs

1 (8 oz.) CHICKEN BREAST, skinned and deboned
1 cup FLOUR
1/4 cup BUTTER
1/2 tsp. minced GARLIC
1 tsp. diced GREEN ONIONS
1 lg. PORTOBELLO MUSHROOM, sliced into strips
1/4 cup DRY RED WINE
1/4 cup BALSAMIC VINEGAR
1/4 cup HALF AND HALF or HEAVY CREAM
3-4 fresh BASIL LEAVES, chopped
SALT and PEPPER
8 oz. WHOLE-WHEAT LINGUINE or SPAGHETTI, cooked

Dredge chicken in flour. Heat skillet over medium heat. When hot, add butter and sauté chicken breast. When chicken is golden brown on one side, add garlic, onions and mushroom. Turn chicken over and brown other side. Add wine and let reduce by half. Add vinegar and let reduce by half again. Add half and half and basil; let reduce and thicken. If needed, add butter. Check for doneness of chicken and flavor of sauce. Season with salt and pepper to taste. Place pasta on serving plate, arrange chicken on top and ladle sauce over all.

Serves 1.

New York Lingo

According to New Yorkers, "upstate" is anything north of New York City, within New York State. Long Island, properly said of course (Lawn Guyland/Lohahn Guylan), is that area of land that lies east of Manhattan (most often meaning Nassau and Suffolk Counties).

Wiener Schnitzel

"This is a favorite recipe that was handed down to me by my grandmother. We serve it often at our home."

Denise Sponholtz—Binghamton

4 (6 oz. ea.) VEAL CUTLETS	SALT and PEPPER
3 Tbsp. FLOUR, divided	1/2 cup MILK
3 Tbsp. grated PARMESAN	6 Tbsp. BUTTER, divided
CHEESE	JUICE of 1 LEMON
1 EGG, beaten	PARSLEY SPRIGS
1 tsp. minced PARSLEY	for garnish
1/4 tsp. NUTMEG	

Wipe meat with damp cloth and pound until very thin. Sprinkle both sides with 1 tablespoon flour. In a medium bowl, mix cheese with remaining flour, egg, parsley, nutmeg and season with salt and pepper to taste. Add milk and beat until smooth. Dip floured cutlets in batter. In a large skillet, cook cutlets over low heat in 4 tablespoons butter until golden brown and tender. Remove cutlets to warm serving platter. Keep hot. In a saucepan, heat remaining butter until it turns dark brown. Add lemon juice, stir and pour over cutlets. Garnish with parsley sprigs.

Serves 4.

Manhattan

The borough of Manhattan is the oldest borough of New York City. Only 13 1/2 miles long and 2 1/3 miles wide, it boasts a population of almost two million and many well-known landmarks and neighborhoods, such as 840-acre Central Park, the Empire State Building, Little Italy, Chinatown, Greenwich Village, Rockefeller Center, the United Nations Headquarters, Harlem, Radio City Music Hall, Times and Herald Squares, to name just a few.

Chicken Fricassee

A New York City, Stage Deli, favorite!

1 (7 lb.) CHICKEN, cut into
  serving pieces
SALT and PEPPER to taste
4 oz. OIL
1 lb. SPANISH ONIONS, diced
2 cloves GARLIC, minced
2 oz. FLOUR
8 oz. DRY WHITE WINE

16 oz. CHICKEN BROTH
2 BAY LEAVES
1 tsp. THYME
1 lb. CARROTS, diced
1 lb. LEEKS, diced
8 oz. HEAVY CREAM
Cooked RICE

Season chicken with salt and pepper, then place in a skillet and sauté for 1 minute without browning. Scatter onions and garlic over chicken and cook, turning often, for 5 minutes. Sprinkle flour over chicken, coating evenly; cook for 5 minutes, turning often. Remove chicken and deglaze skillet with wine. Return chicken to skillet; add chicken broth, bay leaves and thyme. Cover and braise for 30 minutes. Blanch carrots and leeks. When done braising, add cream, carrots and leeks to skillet. Simmer for 2 minutes. Serve over hot rice.

Serves 10.

Barbecued Tenderloin

Marcia Diekmann—Troy

2 Tbsp. BUTTER
1 (2 lb.) BEEF TENDERLOIN STEAK

Marinade:
  1/4 cup chopped GREEN ONIONS
  2 Tbsp. BUTTER
  2 Tbsp. SOY SAUCE

  1 tsp. DIJON MUSTARD
  1/4 tsp. PEPPER
  1/3 cup DRY RED WINE

Spread butter on tenderloin and place in a glass or ceramic dish. In a saucepan, combine marinade ingredients and heat to boiling. Boil for 1 minute, then cool to room temperature. Pour over steak, cover and refrigerate for at least 2 hours. Grill steak, turning every 5 minutes and basting with remaining marinade to preferred doneness.

Serves 8.

Spiedie Sandwiches

Spiedies are native to upstate New York, but can be found wherever New Yorkers may have relocated!

3 lbs. PORK, VENISON, BEEF or skinless CHICKEN BREAST, cut into 1 1/2-inch cubes.

Sauce:

8 crumbled BAY LEAVES	1/2 cup SALAD OIL or
4 tsp. OREGANO	OLIVE OIL
8 sm. cloves GARLIC, minced	1 tsp. PEPPER
1/2 cup LEMON JUICE	3 tsp. SALT
3/4 cup VINEGAR	

FRENCH or ITALIAN BREAD

Combine all sauce ingredients in a glass casserole dish. Add meat, cover and refrigerate for at least 24 hours, stirring occasionally*. Place meat on skewers and grill for five minutes. Serve on large slices of French or Italian bread.

*If using olive oil, remove dish from refrigerator and let set until oil has liquefied. Marinate up to 5 days if desired.

Chicken Curry

Lynda Lumley-Katzman—Sayville

2 lbs. CHICKEN TENDERS	1 jar (24 oz.) APPLESAUCE
1 lg. ONION, diced	2 cans (10.75 oz. ea.) CREAM
4 stalks CELERY, sliced	OF CHICKEN SOUP
4 Tbsp. BUTTER or MARGARINE	1 cup GOLDEN RAISINS
2-3 Tbsp. CURRY	Cooked WHITE RICE
POWDER	Slivered ALMONDS

In a saucepan, cover chicken with water and boil until done. Remove chicken from pan, reserving 1 cup cooking liquid. When chicken has cooled, cut into bite-size pieces. In a large skillet, sauté onion and celery in butter. Add curry powder, stirring well. Stir in applesauce, soup, reserved cooking liquid, raisins and chicken. Cook until heated through. Serve over rice and sprinkle with almonds.

Reuben Sandwiches

Believe it or not, Manhattan (in 1914) and Omaha, Nebraska (in 1925) both lay claim to being the birthplace of the Reuben sandwich!

8 slices RYE or PUMPERNICKEL BREAD
1/2 lb. thinly sliced CORNED BEEF
1 cup well-drained SAUERKRAUT
4 slices SWISS CHEESE
THOUSAND ISLAND DRESSING, if desired
2 Tbsp. BUTTER

Arrange corned beef on tops of 4 of the slices of bread. Pile sauerkraut on top and layer with cheese and dressing. Butter outsides of sandwiches and then grill or broil until bread is browned and cheese melts.

Queens

Queens ranks second in population among New York City's boroughs with a population of nearly two million. Near the Queensboro Bridge, which connects Queens and Manhattan, is Long Island City where much of the borough's industry is concentrated. Forest Hills, La Guardia Airport, John F. Kennedy International Airport, Aqueduct Race Track as well as Shea Stadium and Flushing Meadow Corona Park are all among Queens' landmarks.

Roasted Lamb

6 POTATOES, peeled and sliced	**VEGETABLE SALT**
1 1/2 lbs. LAMB SHOULDER, cubed	**CAYENNE**
1 lg. ONION, sliced	**2 Tbsp. BUTTER, melted**

Place half of potatoes in an oiled casserole dish then add meat. Cover with onion and season with vegetable salt and cayenne to taste. Add remaining potatoes, covering meat completely. Brush with butter. Bake at 350° for 2 hours.

Pasta Fagioli

"On Friday evenings at our home upstate, I serve this dish with a side dish of potatoes and eggs. It's easy to make, filling and delicious."

Concetta Seeno—North Massapequa

3 cloves GARLIC
2 Tbsp. OLIVE OIL
1 can (28 oz.) TOMATO SAUCE
1 can (15 oz.) CANNELLINI BEANS
1/2 tsp. OREGANO
3-4 leaves fresh BASIL LEAVES, chopped
SALT and PEPPER
1/2 lb. DITALINI or other small tube PASTA
Grated PARMESAN CHEESE

In a saucepan, brown garlic in oil over low heat. Add tomato sauce, beans, oregano and basil. Season with salt and pepper to taste. Cover and simmer over low heat, stirring occasionally, for 30 minutes. Cook pasta according to package directions and drain; add 1/2 cup of pasta liquid to bean mixture. In a large bowl, mix together pasta and bean mixture. Top with Parmesan cheese.

Serves 4-5.

Poughkeepsie Chili

3 Tbsp. MARGARINE
1 lg. ONION, diced
1 GREEN BELL PEPPER, diced
1 lb. GROUND BEEF
2 cans (8 oz. ea.) TOMATOES
1 can (10.75 oz.) TOMATO SOUP
1/2 tsp. PAPRIKA
1/8 tsp. CAYENNE
1 BAY LEAF
1 Tbsp. CHILI POWDER
1 clove GARLIC, minced
1 tsp. SALT
2 cans (16 oz. ea.) KIDNEY BEANS

In a skillet or Dutch oven, heat margarine. Add onion, bell pepper and ground beef. Cook until meat is brown, stirring occasionally. Add next 6 ingredients. Cover and simmer about 1 hour, stirring occasionally. Add garlic, salt and beans to mixture. Simmer until thoroughly heated.

Coney Island Hot Dogs

A perfect Coney Island Hot Dog is composed of everything in proportion—so you get a great melding of flavors!

Chili Sauce:

1 Tbsp. BUTTER	1 can (6 oz.) TOMATO SAUCE
1 1/2 lbs. uncooked LEAN GROUND BEEF	1 clove GARLIC, crushed
2 med ONIONS, chopped	6 oz. WATER
1 Tbsp. prepared YELLOW MUSTARD	2 Tbsp. CHILI POWDER
	SALT and PEPPER to taste
	4 or 5 HOT DOGS, ground

HOT DOGS
HOT DOG BUNS
YELLOW MUSTARD
WHITE OR SPANISH ONIONS, chopped
TABASCO®, if desired

Place all sauce ingredients (except ground hot dogs) in a saucepan and simmer until thick. Add ground hot dogs to sauce; cook 15 minutes longer. Place whole hot dogs on buns, place a stripe of mustard along one side. Spread a spoonful of onions on top of the mustard. Spread a spoonful of chili sauce down the opposite side of hot dog. Add Tabasco and then push everything down so you can close the bun. Yum-Yum!

Brooklyn

Brooklyn, the largest of all the New York City boroughs, is home to more than two million people. Brooklyn is connected to Manhattan by the Brooklyn, Manhattan and Williamsburg bridges. Flatbush Avenue begins at the Manhattan Bridge and runs through the heart of the

borough. Brooklyn Heights, Cobble Hill, Prospect Park, Flatbush and Coney Island are some of the well-known places that can be found within this borough.

Rainbow Beef Tenderloin

Butch Kritsberg—Kirkville

1 (3 lb.) BEEF TENDERLOIN ROAST	2 Tbsp. OLIVE OIL
1/4 tsp. crumbled ROSEMARY	2 cloves GARLIC, flattened
SALT and PEPPER	

Preheat oven to 425°. Season meat with rosemary and salt and pepper to taste. In a heavy skillet, heat oil. Sauté garlic until golden; remove. Add meat to skillet and brown; move to a roasting pan. Set skillet aside. Roast meat for 35-45 minutes.

Garnish:
3 oz. dried SHIITAKE MUSHROOMS
2 lg. ONIONS, sliced
2 Tbsp. OLIVE OIL
1 ea. YELLOW, RED and ORANGE BELL PEPPER
3 lg. cloves GARLIC, minced
1 tsp. crumbled ROSEMARY
SALT and PEPPER
1/2 cup fresh PARSLEY, minced

Soak mushrooms for 1/2 hour in hot water, drain and slice. In a skillet, sauté onions in oil until soft. Slice bell peppers, add to skillet and sauté until they begin to soften. Add garlic and rosemary. Stir 1 minute and add mushrooms. Season with salt and pepper to taste. Continue sautéing until mushrooms are tender, about 5 minutes. Stir in parsley.

Gravy:
2 1/2 cups UNSALTED BEEF STOCK, divided
3 Tbsp. GRAND MARNIER LIQUEUR
1 1/2 Tbsp. DIJON MUSTARD
6 Tbsp. BUTTER
SALT and PEPPER
3 Tbsp. fresh PARSLEY, minced

Reheat skillet with drippings. Add 1/2 cup beef stock and bring to a boil, scraping up brown bits. Boil, reducing mixture to a thick syrup, about 8 minutes. Add remaining stock, liqueur and mustard. Continue to boil until thickened. Reduce heat and whisk in butter, one tablespoon at a time. Season with salt and pepper to taste; stir in parsley. Slice meat into 1/2-inch slices, arrange on heated platters and surround with garnish. Serve gravy on the side.

Firecracker Shrimp

Mike Jewell—The Gregory House Country Inn & Restaurant,
Averill Park

Peel and devein **SHRIMP**. Coat shrimp with **CAJUN SEA-SONING**. Coat a heated skillet with **OLIVE OIL**. Add shrimp and sauté until done, about 3-5 minutes. Shrimp will turn from opaque to white. Do not overcook or shrimp will be tough. During the last minute or so of sautéing, add some **HEAVY CREAM**. The amount will depend on the number of servings you're making at one time. Shake in **6-7 drops of TABASCO®**. Remove shrimp from pan and place on a heated serving dish. Add **BUTTER** and **LEMON JUICE** to sauce and let it thicken, stirring frequently. Pour over shrimp and serve.

Did You Know?

Manhattan Island was purchased in 1626 by Peter Minuit, director-general of New Netherland. He paid the Manhattan Indians $24 in trinkets for the island.

Easy Yorkshire Dinner

Rosanne Ehle—Rochester

1 lb. LEAN GROUND BEEF	1 cup FLOUR
1/2 cup chopped ONION	3/4 cup MILK
1/2 cup chopped MUSHROOMS	1 EGG
1 1/2 tsp. SALT, divided	1/2 cup MAYONNAISE
1/4 tsp. PEPPER	

Crumble beef into an 8-inch baking dish. Sprinkle with onion, mushrooms, 1/2 teaspoon salt and pepper. Bake at 425° for 10 minutes; remove. Mix flour and remaining salt together; add milk. Stir until smooth. Beat together egg and mayonnaise; add to flour mixture and mix well. Pour over meat mixture; bake at 425° for 30 minutes or until golden brown. Pour off excess drippings; cut into wedges and serve.

Staten Island Swiss Steak

Jean Hungerford—Guilderland

3 Tbsp. FLOUR
1/4 tsp. SALT
1/4 tsp. PEPPER
1 lb. CUBE STEAK or SIRLOIN, cut into 4 pieces
4 Tbsp. VEGETABLE OIL, divided
1 lg. ONION, thinly sliced
1 lg. stalk CELERY, sliced
1 med. CARROT, very thinly sliced
1 lg. clove GARLIC, minced
1 can (14.5 oz.) STEWED TOMATOES
1/2 cup DRY RED WINE
1 tsp. OREGANO
1 tsp. SAVORY
SALT and PEPPER
Chopped fresh PARSLEY

In a shallow dish, combine flour, salt and pepper; dredge steaks lightly in mixture. Reserve remaining flour mixture. In a heavy skillet, heat 2 tablespoons oil on high heat. Brown steaks 2 minutes per side and transfer to a plate. Add remaining oil to skillet and reduce heat to medium. Add onion, celery and carrot. Cover and cook until vegetables are tender. Add garlic and reserved flour mixture and cook for 1 minute, stirring occasionally. Add tomatoes with liquid, wine, oregano and savory. Return steaks to skillet; bring to a simmer and reduce heat to low. Cook steaks until tender. Add salt and pepper to taste. Place on serving plates; garnish with parsley.

Staten Island

The smallest borough in population (443,770), Staten Island is the only borough not connected to Manhattan by a bridge or tunnel. A ferry from the Staten Island Ferry Terminal at St. George provides the only direct link between the two boroughs. The Staten Island Ferry Harbor Tour passes the Statue of Liberty and provides spectacular views of New York City.

Cajun Chicken Fettuccine

Gordie Hallenbeck—Clifton Park

1 pkg. (12 oz.) FETTUCCINE
1/2 cup BUTTER or EXTRA VIRGIN OLIVE OIL
4 cloves GARLIC, minced
2 bunches GREEN ONIONS, diced
1 lb. boneless CHICKEN, cubed
4 Tbsp. CAJUN SEASONING, divided
1 pkg (12 oz.) MUSHROOMS, chopped
PARMESAN CHEESE

Prepare fettuccine according to package directions. Rinse, drain and set aside. In a skillet, melt butter and sauté garlic and onions until tender. Add chicken and 2 tablespoons cajun seasoning; simmer 3-5 minutes or until chicken is almost done. Add mushrooms. Simmer until mushrooms are tender. Add fettuccine and remaining cajun seasoning. Toss together until well mixed and thoroughly heated. Serve, sprinkled with Parmesan cheese.

Serves 4.

Chile-Tomato Beef Stir-Fry

Frances Kovar—Staten Island

1 lb. (1-inch thick) boneless BEEF
   CHUCK SHOULDER STEAK
1 Tbsp. OLIVE OIL
3 SHALLOTS, thinly sliced
3 CHILE PEPPERS, seeded and sliced
1 clove GARLIC, minced
1 TOMATO, chopped
1/2 cup BEEF BROTH
1 tsp. SOY SAUCE
2 tsp. BROWN SUGAR
CILANTRO SPRIGS
CHERRY TOMATOES

Cut steak into 1/8-inch strips. Heat oil in a wok or wide skillet over medium-high heat. Add half of beef strips; stir-fry for 2 minutes. Remove to warm serving platter. Repeat with remaining meat. Add shallots, peppers and garlic to wok. Stir-fry for 2-3 minutes. Add tomato and cook for 2 minutes. In a bowl, combine beef broth, soy sauce and brown sugar and add to wok. Continue cooking for 1-2 minutes. Pour sauce over beef. Garnish with cilantro sprigs and cherry tomato halves.

Serves 4.

Stuffed Cabbage Leaves

"This is an original recipe. I serve it with mashed potatoes."

Janice Caroli—East Patchogue

1 head CABBAGE
2 lbs. GROUND BEEF
2 EGGS, beaten
1 med. ONION, chopped
2-3 cloves GARLIC, minced
1 cup MINUTE RICE®
1/4 tsp. SALT
Dash of PEPPER
1 can (28 oz.) TOMATO SAUCE, divided
2 BAY LEAVES

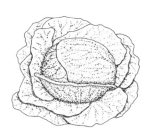

Boil cabbage in a large pot until tender. Remove hot water and replace with cold water; after cabbage has cooled, remove from pot and place in a colander to drain. Cut out core and carefully remove leaves one at a time. A large cabbage should yield 15-20 leaves. Line bottom of pot with 4-5 leaves. In a large bowl, mix ground beef with eggs, onion, garlic, rice, salt, pepper and 1 cup tomato sauce. Place each remaining cabbage leaf with vein facing you on a flat surface and put a small scoop of meat mixture in each center. Roll up leaves, folding in corners. Place them in pot. Pour remaining tomato sauce over cabbage rolls and top with bay leaves. Cover pot and cook over medium heat for 3-4 hours.

Chazy Chicken

New York State Division of Tourism—Albany

1 (2 1/2-3 lb.) CHICKEN, cut up
1/4 cup melted BUTTER
1/2 cup MAPLE SYRUP
1/2 tsp. grated LEMON PEEL
1/2 tsp. SALT
Dash of PEPPER
1/4 cup chopped ALMONDS
2 tsp. LEMON JUICE

Place chicken pieces in a shallow baking pan. Mix remaining ingredients in a bowl and pour evenly over chicken. Bake, uncovered, at 375° for 45-60 minutes, or until tender.

Beef Stroganoff

"This dish can be made ahead of time and reheated."

Charlene Kuhl—Massapequa

2 lbs. LEAN BEEF
FLOUR
1/3 cup MARGARINE, divided
3 med. ONIONS, chopped
1/2 lb. MUSHROOMS, sliced
SALT and PEPPER

2 BEEF BOUILLON CUBES
2 cups HOT WATER
1 can (16 oz.) TOMATO JUICE
1/2 cup SHERRY
2/3 cup SOUR CREAM
Cooked NOODLES

Cut meat into thin strips and dredge in flour. Brown quickly in a skillet in half of the margarine. Remove meat. Add remaining margarine, onions and mushrooms and cook for 5 minutes. Add meat and season with salt and pepper to taste. In a bowl, dissolve bouillon cubes in water; add tomato juice and sherry. Stir into meat mixture. Bring to a boil and simmer for 2 hours or until meat is tender. Just before serving, stir in sour cream. Serve over noodles.

Chicken Marsala

"This is very rich, but so delicious everybody loves it!"

Mary Mingils—Lindenhurst

2 EGGS, well-beaten
2 cups FLOUR
1 lb. CHICKEN BREASTS,
  pounded thin
2 sticks BUTTER
2 sticks MARGARINE
4-5 cloves GARLIC, minced

10 oz. MUSHROOMS, sliced
1-2 ONIONS, diced
2 tsp. PARSLEY
1 Tbsp. LEMON JUICE
1/2 cup WINE
SALT and PEPPER
Cooked WHITE RICE

Place eggs in a shallow dish. Place flour on a plate. Dip chicken in eggs, then dredge in flour. Melt 1 stick butter and 1 stick margarine in a skillet. Fry chicken until golden brown on both sides; place in casserole dish. In the same skillet, melt remaining butter and margarine. Sauté garlic, mushrooms and onion until tender. Add parsley, lemon juice and wine; season with salt and pepper to taste. Pour over chicken. Cover and bake at 325° for 30 minutes. Serve over rice.

Fran's Great One-Pot Meal

"I make this for almost every occasion."

Frances Cosby—Farmingdale

2 Tbsp. OIL	SALT and PEPPER
1 GREEN BELL PEPPER,	1 1/2 lbs. BEEFSTEAK, sliced
thinly sliced	2 cans (15 oz. ea.) SLICED
1 RED BELL PEPPER,	POTATOES, undrained
thinly sliced	1 can (14.5 oz.) CUT GREEN
1/2 ONION, thinly sliced	BEANS, undrained
OREGANO	1 can (15 oz.) TOMATO SAUCE
GARLIC POWDER	Cooked WHITE RICE
BASIL	ITALIAN BREAD, sliced

Heat oil in a large skillet. Add bell peppers, onion and seasonings to taste; sauté until vegetables are soft. Remove from skillet and add steak, cooking until browned on both sides. Stir in potatoes and green beans with liquids and tomato sauce. Cover and simmer for 30 minutes. Return vegetable mixture to skillet and heat through. Serve over rice with Italian bread on the side.

Steak Pizzaiola

"The secret ingredient in this recipe is the Gravy Master®. It gives the tomato sauce a dark, rich color."

Concetta Seeno—North Massapequa

1 (2 lb.) CHUCK STEAK	1/2 tsp. GRAVY MASTER®
4 cloves GARLIC, minced	SALT and PEPPER
2 Tbsp. OLIVE OIL	OREGANO
1 can (28 oz.) TOMATOES	4 fresh BASIL LEAVES
1/4-1/2 can WATER	

Place steak in a large baking dish. In a medium bowl, mix remaining ingredients and pour over steak. Cover tightly with foil and bake at 325° for 1 1/2 hours.

Stuffed Breast of Veal

"The Metronome Restaurant is situated in a landmark building on Broadway. A Gothic entrance leads to the 1920s and 1930s inspired dining area that features many architectural delights."

Chef Robert Cangelosi—Metronome Restaurant, New York City

1 boneless BREAST OF VEAL

Stuffing:
    2 oz. dried PORCINI MUSHROOMS, soaked
      in cool water for 2 hours
    2 Tbsp. finely chopped GARLIC
    2 tsp. OLIVE OIL
    1 1/2 lbs. LEAN GROUND VEAL
    SALT and PEPPER
    1 EGG
    2 1/2 cups HEAVY CREAM
    1 bunch SPINACH, blanched and
      finely chopped
    1 bunch fresh SAGE, finely chopped

3 lg. ONIONS, coarsely diced	SALT and PEPPER
3 lg. CARROTS, coarsely diced	1 1/2 cups MADEIRA WINE
2 bulbs GARLIC, separated	8 cups VEAL or BEEF STOCK

Remove fat from veal breast and lightly pound to 1-inch thick with meat mallet; set aside. To prepare stuffing: Drain mushrooms and sauté with garlic in oil; set aside. In a food processor, mix ground veal seasoned with salt and pepper to taste for 30 seconds. Add egg and process until veal forms into a ball. With machine running, slowly add cream. Transfer mixture to a bowl and add spinach, sage and mushroom mixture. Spread stuffing over veal, then roll and tie with butcher's string at 1-inch increments. Place onions, carrots and garlic in a roasting pan. Lay stuffed veal breast on top. Lightly oil and season veal with salt and pepper to taste. Cook at 340° for 1 1/2 hours, or until tender; let sit for 20 minutes, then remove from pan. Add wine and stock to roasting pan. Bring to a boil, then simmer for 20 minutes to thicken; strain. Season sauce with salt and pepper to taste. Remove string from veal and slice. Serve with sauce on the side.

New York-Style Pizza

Once called a "tomato pie", today's New York-style pizza retains its 100-year-old place in the history of America.

Pizza Dough:
1 tsp. ACTIVE DRY YEAST
2/3 cup WARM WATER
2 cups FLOUR
1 tsp. SALT
2 Tbsp. OLIVE OIL

2 cups TOMATO SAUCE
1 lb. MOZZARELLA, thinly sliced
1/2 cup grated ROMANO CHEESE
1/4 cup chopped fresh BASIL
1 Tbsp. OREGANO
1 tsp. RED PEPPER FLAKES
2 Tbsp. OLIVE OIL

Combine yeast and water and let stand for 1 minute. Stir until dissolved. In a bowl, combine flour, salt and olive oil. Stir in yeast mixture. Continue stirring until a soft dough forms, then knead for 5 minutes, adding more flour if dough is too sticky. Form dough into a ball. Coat a bowl with oil, add dough and cover tightly with plastic wrap. Let rise for 1 1/2 hours. Place dough on a very lightly floured board and roll out to a diameter of 12-inches. Place on pizza stone or round pizza pan. Spread tomato sauce evenly over dough. Sprinkle with mozzarella and Romano cheese, basil, oregano and pepper flakes. Drizzle top with olive oil. Bake pizza on bottom shelf of a 475° oven for 12-15 minutes or until crispy and cheese bubbles.

Pizza Time Line

- *Spaniards introduced the tomato to Italy in the 16th century.*
- *The original mozzarella cheese was made from the milk of the Indian water buffalo in the 7th century. It was introduced to Italy in the 18th century.*
- *The world's first pizzeria opened in Naples, Italy in 1830.*
- *An Italian immigrant named Gennaro Lombardi opened the first U. S. pizzeria in 1895 in New York City.*

Chinese Pork & Noodles

Popular in Chinese, Thai and other Asian cuisines, cellophane noodles (also known as bean thread, harusame, or glass noodles) are fine, dry, transparent noodles made from green mung bean paste (starch).

4 oz. CELLOPHANE NOODLES
1/2 lb. coarsely ground PORK TENDERLOIN
2 Tbsp. SESAME OIL
1/4 lb. CARROTS, grated
1 can (8 oz.) WATER CHESTNUTS,
    drained and chopped
1 Tbsp. HOISIN SAUCE
1/2 cup CHICKEN STOCK
1 clove GARLIC, minced
1 Tbsp. coarsely grated GINGER
2 Tbsp. DRY SHERRY
1 Tbsp. SOY SAUCE
2 GREEN ONIONS, sliced

Add noodles to a bowl and enough hot water to cover; soak for 10 minutes. In a large skillet, heat 1 tablespoon sesame oil; add ground tenderloin and cook only until meat is no longer pink. Remove meat from skillet and set aside. Add remaining tablespoon oil to skillet; stir in carrots and sauté until slightly tender. Add all remaining ingredients except green onions and return meat to pan. Bring to a simmer and cook 2-3 minutes. Drain noodles, cut into bite size lengths and stir into pork mixture until well coated. Serve, garnished with green onions.

Madison Square Garden

Madison Square Garden, located near bustling Pennsylvania Station in Manhattan, is home to professional basketball teams the Knicks and the Liberty, as well as the New York Rangers hockey team. The facility hosts several other sports events including collegiate tournaments as well as various entertainment acts; it has long been regarded as a major venue for world-famous performers.

SIDE DISHES

Niagara Falls

Niagara Falls is on the Niagara River, about halfway between Lakes Erie and Ontario. The Falls actually consist of two waterfalls: Horseshoe Falls in the province of Ontario, Canada, and American Falls in the state of New York. Cave of the Winds was carved behind the American Falls by the pounding water. A trip on "The Maid of the Mist" takes sightseers close to the churning waters at the base of the falls. Niagara Falls is a favorite destination for honeymooners.

★ ★ ★ ★ *Cooking Across America* ★ ★ ★ ★

Goat Cheese & Leek Tart

"Nestled in the heart of the majestic Adirondack Mountains lies the village of Saranac Lake. It is here that you will find the historic Hotel Saranac of Paul Smith's College."

Chef John McBride—Hotel Saranac of Paul Smith's College,
Saranac Lake

Pastry:
- 1 cup FLOUR
- 1 tsp. SALT
- 4 oz. UNSALTED BUTTER
- 1 EGG
- 1 Tbsp. ICE WATER

In a mixing bowl, combine flour and salt. Cut in butter until mixture resembles coarse cornmeal. Combine egg with water. Add just enough egg mixture to the flour mixture to create a dough. Wrap in plastic wrap and refrigerate for 1 hour.

Filling:
- 2 cups LEEKS (white part only)
- BUTTER
- 8 oz. GOAT CHEESE
- 4 oz. CREAM CHEESE
- 2 Tbsp. HEAVY CREAM
- 2 EGGS
- Pinch of NUTMEG
- SALT and PEPPER

Preheat oven to 375°. Julienne leeks and sweat in butter. In a bowl, combine cheeses, cream, eggs and nutmeg. Season with salt and pepper to taste. Add 1 cup leeks and combine.

Roll out pastry dough and place in a 9-inch tart pan. Trim off excess dough. Pour leek mixture into shell. Top with remaining leeks and bake for 20 minutes or until golden brown.

Apple & Brown Rice Pilaf

- 1/2 ONION, minced
- 1 Tbsp. VEGETABLE OIL
- 1 1/2 cups QUICK COOKING BROWN RICE
- 1 1/4 cups CHICKEN BROTH
- 1/2 tsp. dried THYME
- SALT and PEPPER
- 2 cups RED DELICIOUS APPLES, cored and diced
- 2 Tbsp. chopped PARSLEY

In a skillet, sauté onion in oil until tender. Stir in rice and brown slightly. Add broth, thyme, salt and pepper to taste. Bring mixture to a boil, then cover tightly and reduce heat; simmer for 15 minutes. Stir in apples and parsley and serve.

Lokshen Kugel
(Noodle Pudding)

"Through countless Shabbat dinners, Ashkenazic Jews have eaten some type of kugel, the Yiddish term for pudding. It can be made from noodles, potatoes, apples, carrots, rice or even matzoh, all held together by eggs then baked golden brown. Although some cooks enrich their lokshen kugels with cottage cheese, cream cheese, and / or sour cream, this is a pareve version to go with a meat-based menu."

The Kosher Gourmet Cookbook—New York City

1 pkg. (16 oz.) BROAD EGG NOODLES
2 sticks MARGARINE, melted
1 cup SUGAR
4 EGGS, beaten
1 APPLE, peeled and grated
1/2 cup GOLDEN RAISINS
1 Tbsp. ORANGE MARMALADE
1 tsp. VANILLA EXTRACT
Ground CINNAMON

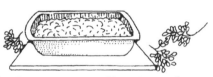

Cook noodles in boiling, salted water according to package directions; drain. Preheat oven to 375°. Grease a 13 x 9 baking dish. In a large bowl, combine drained noodles with remaining ingredients except cinnamon; mix well. Pour into prepared baking dish, smoothing top. Sprinkle with cinnamon. Bake kugel about 1 hour or until golden and set.

Twice-Baked Potatoes

Marion Robinson—Guilderland

4 med. POTATOES, baked
1 cup LOW FAT COTTAGE CHEESE
1/2 cup LOW FAT MILK
1 Tbsp. minced ONION

Dash of PEPPER
Dash of PAPRIKA
Dash of PARSLEY
    FLAKES

Cut potatoes in half. Scoop out potato leaving skins intact. Beat potatoes with cottage cheese, milk and onion. Spoon potato mixture back into skins and sprinkle with seasonings. Bake at 350° for 10 minutes or until golden brown.

Saratoga Potato Chips

According to one story, the potato chip was born at Moon's Lake House on Saratoga Lake, New York in 1853. Aunt Kate, an Indian cook, was bustling around the kitchen where, like most cooks at dinner time, she was trying to do a number of things at the same time. One of her activities involved slicing potatoes and in the confusion, one slice dropped into a pan of hot fat. By the time Aunt Kate was able to fish the slice out, it had cooked to a delicious golden brown. A hungry guest passing through the kitchen popped it into his mouth and ordered more. For years the chips were known as Saratoga chips but eventually, as they were enjoyed from coast to coast, the name was changed to "potato chips."

New York State Division of Tourism—Albany

Pare **POTATOES,** slice into thin shavings with a vegetable cutter and soak in **ICE WATER** for one hour. Remove from water and dry on paper towels. Fry potatoes in **OIL** until they curl and are delicately brown. Be careful that the oil is not too hot, as the potatoes must cook before they brown. Shake as much oil from potatoes as possible and place on paper towels to drain. Dust with **SALT.** Allow oil to reheat before adding more potatoes.

 An Illuminating Fact! *The first all-electric house was built in 1903 in Schenectady.*

Summer Squash Casserole

Helen Mac Gregor—Guilderland

YELLOW SUMMER SQUASH, sliced and stewed
2 Tbsp. BUTTER
1/2 cup shredded CHEDDAR CHEESE
GARLIC SALT

Mix squash with butter, cheese and season with garlic salt to taste. Put squash mixture into a casserole dish. Cover and bake for 45 minutes at 325°.

German-Style Cooked Cabbage & Apples

8 cups shredded RED or GREEN CABBAGE
5 cups peeled and sliced CORTLAND APPLES
4 cups BOILING, SALTED WATER
4 slices BACON, diced
1 cup sliced ONION
2 Tbsp. CIDER VINEGAR
2 Tbsp. SUGAR
1/2 tsp. dried FENNEL SEED, crushed
1/4 tsp. GROUND BLACK PEPPER

In a large saucepan, combine cabbage, apples and water; simmer for 5 minutes or until cabbage is barely tender. Drain well and then place in a serving bowl. In a skillet, fry bacon and onion until onion is tender; stir in remaining ingredients and cook for 2 minutes. Add bacon mixture to cabbage mixture and mix lightly.

About Cooking Apples
Cortland, Baldwin, Northern Spy, Rome Beauty, Winesap and York Imperial are all good cooking and baking apples. They remain flavorful and firm throughout the process.

Creamy Carrot Casserole

Shirley Breigle—Windham

1 1/2 lbs. CARROTS, sliced
1/2 cup MAYONNAISE
2 Tbsp. chopped ONION
2 Tbsp. HORSERADISH

1/4 tsp. SALT
Dash of PEPPER
1/4 cup crushed SALTINES
2 Tbsp. BUTTER

In a saucepan, cook carrots in enough water to cover until tender; drain. While carrots are hot, mix in mayonnaise, onion, horseradish and seasonings. Put in a casserole dish, top with saltines and dot with butter. Bake at 350° for 30 minutes.

Zucchini "Stuff"

"This recipe was given to me by a neighbor. She said the recipe was never written, just handed down through the family. Whenever I make it everyone just loves it!"

Eileen Giannico—Bethpage

2 med. ONIONS, coarsely chopped
2 Tbsp. OIL
1 med. ZUCCHINI, sliced 1/4-inch thick
1 lg. clove GARLIC, minced
1 can (16 oz.) CRUSHED or STEWED TOMATOES or
    5 med. TOMATOES, chopped
1/2 tsp. OREGANO
1 Tbsp. BASIL or 5 fresh BASIL LEAVES, chopped
2 tsp. SUGAR
SALT and PEPPER
2 cups shredded MOZZARELLA CHEESE

Sauté onions in oil until translucent. Add zucchini and garlic and sauté 6 minutes or until zucchini is tender. Add tomatoes, oregano, basil and sugar. Season with salt and pepper to taste. Cook, covered, about 10 minutes. Remove cover and simmer until thick. When done, sprinkle with cheese and simmer until melted.

Chantilly Potatoes

"These potatoes are perfect with baked ham."

Dottie Gralow—Guilderland

4-6 POTATOES
1/4-1/2 cup MILK
BUTTER
SALT and PEPPER

1/2 cup CREAM
1/2 cup grated CHEDDAR
    CHEESE

Cook, drain and mash potatoes to measure 3-4 cups. Add enough milk to make potatoes light and fluffy. Stir in butter and salt and pepper to taste. Beat well. Place in a greased casserole dish. In a bowl, whip cream until stiff. Fold in cheese. Spread cream mixture on potatoes and bake in a 350° oven for 15 minutes or until lightly browned.

Schenectady Squash with Walnut Filling

"This makes a good Thanksgiving main course for vegetarians. It is also an excellent side dish for any meal!"

Deb Fish—Schenectady

2 med. ACORN or BUTTERNUT SQUASH
OIL

Split squash lengthwise down the middle. Remove seeds and bake in a 350° oven, face down, on an oiled baking pan for 30 minutes. Pack *Walnut Filling* into squash cavities. Cover with foil and bake at 350° for 25 minutes.

Walnut Filling

3-4 Tbsp. BUTTER
Pinch of SALT
1/2 cup chopped ONION
1 lg. clove GARLIC, minced
1 stalk CELERY, chopped
1/4 cup chopped WALNUTS
1/4 cup SUNFLOWER SEEDS
SALT and PEPPER

1/2 tsp. rubbed SAGE
1/2 tsp. THYME
1 cup coarsely crumbled
    WHOLE-WHEAT BREAD
JUICE of 1/2 LEMON
1/4 cup RAISINS, optional
1/2 cup grated CHEDDAR
    CHEESE

In a skillet, heat butter and salt. Sauté onion, garlic, celery, walnuts and seeds. Cook over low heat until onion is translucent, nuts are browned and celery is tender. Season with salt and pepper to taste. Add remaining ingredients, except cheese. Cook, stirring over low heat for 5-8 minutes. Remove from heat and mix in cheese.

Schenectady

Schenectady has been called the "City that Lights and Hauls the World" because it had huge electrical-manufacturing and locomotive industries. A new exhibit "The Spirit of Schenectady" at the Schenectady Museum showcases the inventions and innovations that happened here.

Mashed Potatoes & Turnips

Lisa Kennedy—Schenectady

1 lg. TURNIP, peeled and diced
8 med. POTATOES, peeled and diced
1 lg. ONION, diced
1/4 cup MILK
SALT and PEPPER
1 cup shredded SHARP CHEDDAR CHEESE, divided

In a saucepan, boil together turnip, potatoes and onion until soft. Mash, blending in milk. Season with salt and pepper to taste. Add 3/4 cup cheese and mix well. Place in a greased baking dish. Top with remaining cheese. Bake at 350° until warmed through and cheese is melted and bubbly.

The Empire State

Some historians believe that New York's nickname—the Empire State—came from a remark made by George Washington when he visited New York in 1783 and predicted that it might become the seat of a new empire.

Green Beans & Peppers

Diane Pikul—Schenectady

1 lb. GREEN BEANS
1/2 cup julienne RED BELL PEPPER
1/2 cup julienne YELLOW BELL PEPPER
1/2 cup sliced ONION
2 cloves GARLIC, minced
2 Tbsp. MARGARINE
SALT and PEPPER

In a large skillet, sauté beans, bell peppers, onion and garlic in margarine for 6-8 minutes or until just tender. Season with salt and pepper to taste.

Spanish Ratatouille

(Ra-tuh-TOO-ee)

'This dish is often served at gatherings of my father's family, who emigrated from Spain before WWI. It is best cooked in a heavy cast iron skillet and can be served hot or cold."

Juanita R. Vazquez—Amityville

5-6 RED BELL PEPPERS
1 GREEN BELL PEPPER
1 ORANGE BELL PEPPER
1 YELLOW BELL PEPPER
2 VIDALIA ONIONS
LIGHT OLIVE OIL
3 cloves GARLIC, coarsely minced
1 1/2 cups YELLOW RAISINS
1 can (6 oz.) pitted BLACK OLIVES, sliced
Freshly ground PEPPER

Core and slice bell peppers into strips about 1/2-inch wide; slice onions into 1/4-inch sections. Thickly coat a hot skillet with olive oil and allow oil to heat. Add peppers and sauté for 8 minutes, then add onions and cook for another 20-25 minutes. Add garlic and cook for 10 minutes or until thoroughly cooked. Remove from heat. Add raisins and olives. Season with pepper to taste. Let sit for half an hour before serving.

Zucchini Tomato Sauce

"I usually serve this over buttered noodles."

Connie Puma—Wantagh

3 ZUCCHINI, sliced
2 Tbsp. BUTTER
2 cups chopped TOMATOES
SALT and PEPPER
1 cup grated MOZZARELLA CHEESE

Sauté zucchini in butter until tender. Add tomatoes and season with salt and pepper to taste. Cook until tomatoes are tender, about 10 minutes. Add cheese and cook until melted.

English Stilton Fritters

"You'll think you're in England when you approach the entrance to this restaurant—it's lined with red telephone booths!"

Chef Stacey Ference—Telephone Bar & Grill, New York City

1 lb. CREAM CHEESE	2 cups PLAIN BREAD
1 lb. ENGLISH STILTON CHEESE	CRUMBS
4 EGGS, beaten	OIL for frying

In a food processor, mix cheeses until just blended. Do not cream. Refrigerate until firm, then roll into 1 1/2-inch balls. Refrigerate again until firm. Dip balls, one at a time, into eggs and roll in bread crumbs. Keep balls refrigerated until ready to cook. Deep fry until golden brown and serve immediately with *Cranberry Relish* on the side.

Cranberry Relish

2 cups CRANBERRIES
1 ORANGE, unpeeled, cut into wedges and seeded
1 cup SUGAR

Blend all ingredients in a food processor until smooth.

New York and the Revolution
One third of all battles of the Revolutionary War were fought in New York.

Sunseas Topping

"This flavorful topping is great on pasta, pizza and salads."

Ali Dorian—*New York New Wave Health Recipes*, Staten Island

8 oz. UNSALTED SUNFLOWER SEEDS
2 Tbsp. SWEET BASIL
1/2 tsp. WHITE PEPPER
1/2 tsp. SEA SALT
1/2 Tbsp. crushed RED PEPPER

Combine all ingredients in a blender or food processor and process until moderately fine. Keep refrigerated.

The Adirondacks

Stretching over 6 million acres, the Adirondacks provide more than 2,000 lakes and ponds as well as 46 peaks that are over 4,000 feet tall. Lakes Champlain and George form the eastern border of this region while the Mohawk and St. Lawrence river valleys define its southern and northern limits. Lake Placid and the highest skiing peak in the East, Whiteface Mountain, lie in the northern part of this range. The Adirondacks provide an opportunity for a wide variety of hiking, skiing, boating, river running and other outdoor activities.

Herb Bread

Michael K. Anderson—Rochester

1/2 cup chopped ONION
1 clove GARLIC, minced
1 tsp. BASIL
1 Tbsp. BUTTER
1 EGG, beaten
1/2 cup MILK

1/2 cup BISCUIT MIX
1 cup shredded ROMANO
   or ASIAGO CHEESE
1 tsp. minced DILL
1/4 cup melted BUTTER

Sauté onion, garlic and basil in butter until tender. In a bowl, combine egg and milk. Fold in biscuit mix and stir until blended. Add onion mixture and 1/2 of the cheese. Stir to combine. Spread dough in an 8-inch round baking dish. Sprinkle top with remaining cheese. Sprinkle dill over cheese and top with melted butter. May be refrigerated for up to 24 hours before baking. Bake at 400° for 20-25 minutes. Cut into triangles and serve warm.

Albany

Albany was chosen as the state's capital in 1797. Originally a settlement named Beverwyck, Albany was renamed in honor of the English Duke of York and Albany.

Zucchini Bread

Eileen Giannico—Bethpage

3 cups grated ZUCCHINI
2 1/2 cups SUGAR
1 cup OIL
1 cup WALNUTS
1 1/2 tsp. CINNAMON

4 EGGS, slightly beaten
3 cups FLOUR
2 tsp. BAKING POWDER
1 tsp. BAKING SODA
1 tsp. SALT

In a large bowl, mix together all ingredients. Place batter in a greased and floured 13 x 9 baking pan or 2 large loaf pans and bake for 1 hour at 350°.

Note: Raisins that have been soaked in rum may be added.

Apricot Bran Muffins

Jerry Mohr—Guilderland

2 cups FLOUR
1 1/4 cups packed BROWN
 SUGAR
1 cup BRAN CEREAL
2 tsp. BAKING POWDER
1 tsp. BAKING SODA
1/2 tsp. SALT
1 cup RAISINS

1/2 cup chopped DRIED
 APRICOTS
1 EGG
1 cup SOUR CREAM
1/2 cup VEGETABLE OIL
1/2 cup frozen ORANGE
 JUICE CONCENTRATE

In a bowl, mix together flour, sugar, cereal, baking powder, baking soda and salt. Stir in raisins and apricots. In another bowl, beat the egg. Stir in sour cream, oil, and thawed orange juice. Combine with dry ingredients just until moistened. Spoon batter into lined large muffin cups. Fill cups to top of liner. Bake at 375° for 20 minutes or until firm to the touch.

Makes 16 muffins.

♥♥♥
I Love New York Scones

"I make these scones for a local gourmet coffee and chocolate shop called Sweet Attitudes."

Wanda G. Dean—Wellsville

5 1/4 cups sifted FLOUR
1 cup BUTTER
3/4 cup SUGAR
7 1/2 tsp. BAKING POWDER
1 1/2 tsp. SALT

3 EGGS, slightly beaten
1 cup HEAVY CREAM
1 Tbsp. VANILLA
1 1/2 cups dried CURRANTS

Process flour, butter, sugar, baking powder and salt in a food processor to cornmeal consistency. In a bowl, combine eggs, cream and vanilla. Add flour mixture and currants and mix together with a wooden spoon. Roll out onto a floured board to 1/3-inch thickness. Cut into heart shapes and sprinkle with sugar. Bake at 400° for 10-12 minutes or until lightly browned on the bottoms.

New York State's Official
Apple Muffins

These treats were created by Jillann Motto for the Bear Road Elementary School in North Syracuse. Governor Mario Cuomo signed a bill making this the official state muffin.

New York Division of Tourism—Albany

2 cups FLOUR
3/4 cup packed BROWN
   SUGAR
1/2 cup SUGAR
2 tsp. BAKING SODA
1/2 tsp. SALT
1 1/2 tsp. CINNAMON
1/2 tsp. CLOVES

1/8 tsp. NUTMEG
2 cups chopped APPLES
1/2 cup RAISINS
1/2 cup chopped WALNUTS
3 EGGS, slightly beaten
1/2 cup melted BUTTER
4 oz. CREAM CHEESE, diced
1/2 tsp. VANILLA

In a bowl, combine flour, sugars, baking soda and salt and set aside. In another bowl, combine remaining ingredients and mix well. Add flour mixture to apple mixture a little at a time, stirring until just combined. Spoon batter into lined muffin cups; sprinkle with *Walnut Topping.* Bake at 375° for 20-25 minutes or until golden brown.

Walnut Topping

1/4 cup FLOUR
1 tsp. CINNAMON
1/2 cup chopped WALNUTS

1/2 cup packed BROWN SUGAR
1 tsp. grated LEMON PEEL
2 Tbsp. melted BUTTER

In a bowl, combine all topping ingredients.

Rochester

Rochester lies near the Genesee River's outlet to Lake Ontario. Originally incorporated as Rochesterville in 1817, Rochester received a city charter in 1834. Rochester is nicknamed "Film City" because the Eastman Kodak Company, a leading manufacturer of cameras and film, is headquartered there. The city became an ocean port in 1959 when the St. Lawrence Seaway opened.

New York Bagels

What sets bagels apart from other breads is that they are quickly boiled before being baked, resulting in a dense, chewy texture. While variations are endless, this is a good basic recipe.

1 1/2 cups WARM WATER	1 Tbsp. SALT
2 1/2 tsp. YEAST	4 1/2 - 5 1/2 cups FLOUR
1 Tbsp. SUGAR	2 Tbsp. MOLASSES

In a large bowl, combine 1/4 cup warm water with the yeast and 1 teaspoon sugar. Stir to dissolve; let stand for 5 minutes or until foamy. Stir in remaining water, sugar, salt and about 4 cups of flour. Mix until well combined. Mix in portions of the remaining flour until dough is no longer sticky. Turn dough onto a lightly-floured surface and knead until smooth and elastic (5-8 minutes). Shape dough into a ball; place in a greased bowl; cover with a towel and let rise until doubled (about 1 1/2 hours). Punch dough down and divide into 12 pieces. Return to bowl and cover with towel; let rest for 20 minutes. With floured hands, roll each piece of dough into a 12-14 inch rope. Wrap ropes into circles and pinch ends together. Preheat oven to 375°. Bring a large pot of water to a boil; stir in molasses. Drop two bagels into the water and cook them for about 20 seconds. Using a slotted spoon, transfer bagels to an ungreased baking sheet. Continue with remaining bagels. Sprinkle with toppings of choice and bake for about 20 minutes, or until crusty and browned.

Bagel History

The art of bagel-making was once a closely guarded secret. The International Beigel Bakers' Union was founded in New York City in 1907 (now disbanded), with regulations that permitted only sons of members as apprentices. In 1927, Polish baker Harry Lender went to New Haven, CT and founded the first bagel factory outside New York City.

Round Challahs

Challah has played an integral role in Jewish tradition since biblical times. Portions of bread dough, the challah, were given to priests: "Of the first of your dough you shall set apart a cake for a gift" (Numbers 15:20). Since white flour was the choice of the wealthy, it was used in the Shabbat and holiday loaves. Today, challah refers to the Sabbath loaves. To keep up with progress, this recipe was developed for the food processor to save time, but it can also be mixed in a large bowl.

The Kosher Gourmet Cookbook—New York City

2 pkgs. (.25 oz. ea.) ACTIVE DRY
 YEAST
6-8 cups FLOUR, divided
1/2 cup SUGAR
1 Tbsp. SALT

1/2 cup MARGARINE
1 3/4 cups + 2 Tbsp. WATER,
 divided
5 EGGS, divided
POPPY or SESAME SEEDS

Combine yeast, 3 cups flour, sugar and salt in a food processor. In a saucepan, heat margarine and 1 3/4 cups water over medium heat to about 110° on thermometer (liquid should feel hot but not burn your finger). Add margarine mixture to yeast mixture in processor; cover and process until blended. With machine running, add 4 eggs, one at a time, until blended. Gradually add enough remaining flour through the feed tube to form a ball of dough that cleans the sides of the container. Process dough around container 25 times.

On a lightly-floured surface, knead dough 10-15 times, until smooth and elastic. Place in a greased bowl, turning to grease sides. Cover with towel and let rise about 1 hour or until dough has doubled in size.

Punch dough down and divide into 3 pieces. Cover and let rest 10 minutes. Roll each piece into ropes about 1 1/2-inches in diameter. Coil each rope into a circle. Place circles on greased cookie sheets; cover and let rise about 45 minutes or until doubled in size (or cover and let rise overnight in refrigerator). Preheat oven to 350°. In a bowl, beat remaining egg

(Continued on next page)

70 *Breads*

(**Round Challahs** *(continued from previous page)*) with 2 tablespoons water. Brush challahs with egg mixture; sprinkle with poppy seeds. Bake for 40-50 minutes, until golden brown and hollow-sounding when tapped with fingers. Remove to wire racks to cool.

Note: To make challah rolls, divide dough into small balls and shape into coils or braids. Bake on a greased cookie sheet, spaced at least 2-inches apart, at 375° for 20-25 minutes.

The Finger Lakes

The Finger Lakes, which were created by the glaciers of the Ice Age, consist of eleven bodies of water. The lakes, all of which are long and narrow, lie nearly parallel in a north-south direction. The beauty of the Finger Lakes region is marked by lush forests, rolling hills and cascading waterfalls. The majesty is enhanced by the presence of several nationally recognized wineries. In fact, the Finger Lakes region is America's largest wine-producing region outside of California.

Irish Soda Bread

"We have enjoyed this bread for years after attending the St. Patrick's Day parade."

Wanda G. Dean—Wellsville

1 1/2 cups dried CURRANTS	2 tsp. BAKING SODA
1/2 cup IRISH WHISKEY	2 tsp. BAKING POWDER
6 Tbsp. BUTTER, softened	1 1/4 tsp. SALT
5 cups FLOUR	Grated PEEL of 2 ORANGES
6 Tbsp. SUGAR	1 1/2 cups BUTTERMILK

Soak currants for 1/2 hour in whiskey; drain. Place next six ingredients in a food proccessor and process to cornmeal consistency. Place flour mixture in a mixing bowl and stir in orange peel and buttermilk. Add currants and mix thoroughly. Shape into 2 round loaves. Cut an "X" on the top about 1/4-inch deep with a floured sharp knife. Bake on greased baking pans at 375° for 45-60 minutes.

Pumpkin Bread

Eileen Giannico—Bethpage

2 1/2 cups SUGAR
3 1/3 cups FLOUR
2 tsp. BAKING SODA
1 1/2 tsp. SALT
3 tsp. CINNAMON

3 tsp. NUTMEG
1 cup OIL
4 EGGS, slightly beaten
2 cups PUMPKIN
2/3 cup WATER

Combine all dry ingredients by hand in a large bowl. Add remaining ingredients and mix well. Mixture will be lumpy. Place batter in a 13 x 9 greased and floured pan or 2 large loaf pans and bake at 350° for 1 hour.

Note: Add nuts and/or rum-soaked raisins for variety.

Ithaca

Ithaca is at the southern tip of Cayuga Lake in the Finger Lakes Region. This region is home to the beautiful Buttermilk and Taughannock Falls. Nearby Robert C. Treman State Park offers many recreational opportunities. The Cayuga Wine Trail heads north, leading to more than a dozen wineries along the way.

Hobo Bread

"Start this bread the night before house guests arrive. As the bread bakes in the early morning, the aroma will greet them when they awaken."

Sara Schmidt—The Marshall House, Schuylerville

2 cups RAISINS
2 1/2 cups BOILING WATER
4 tsp. BAKING SODA
1 cup packed BROWN SUGAR
1 cup WHITE SUGAR

4 Tbsp. OIL
4 cups FLOUR
1/4 tsp. SALT
NUTS or FRUIT, optional

In a bowl, combine raisins, water and baking soda and soak overnight. The next morning, in a large bowl, combine all ingredients and mix well. Grease and flour 3 (1-pound) coffee cans and fill each half full. Bake for 70 minutes at 325°. Cool 15-20 minutes before removing from cans.

The Catskills

Early American Indians called this heavily-forested area "Onteora," or "land in the sky." Forming a chain of low mountains along the western shore of the Hudson River, the Catskills are about 50 miles long and 30 miles wide. Highest peaks include Slide Mountain and Hunter Mountain—both are over 4,000 feet high. The Catskills are one of the most beautiful natural regions in New York.

Classic New York Cheesecake

A good New York cheesecake should be tall, dense and chewy. Most New York cheesecakes are not topped with anything, but feel free to add a light touch of berries and sauce!

Crust:
   1 cup GRAHAM CRACKER CRUMBS
   3 Tbsp. SUGAR
   1/2 tsp. CINNAMON
   3 Tbsp. BUTTER or MARGARINE, melted

Filling:
   5 pkgs. (8 oz. ea.) CREAM
      CHEESE, softened
   1 cup SUGAR
   3 Tbsp. FLOUR
   1 Tbsp. VANILLA
   3 EGGS
   1 cup SOUR CREAM

To make crust: In a bowl, combine cracker crumbs, sugar, cinnamon and butter. Press mixture onto bottom of a 9-inch springform pan using the bottom of a straight-sided glass to press mixture evenly. Bake crust at 350° for 10 minutes. To make filling: In a mixing bowl, combine cream cheese, sugar, flour and vanilla. Using an electric mixer on medium speed, mix until well-blended. Add eggs, one at a time, mixing on low speed after each addition just until blended. Blend in sour cream. Pour cream cheese mixture into crust and bake at 350° for 1 hour or until center is almost set. Remove pan from oven and run a knife or metal spatula around rim to loosen cake. Cool before removing rim from pan. Refrigerate cake 4 hours or overnight.

Did You Know?

In 1872, cream cheese was invented by American dairymen who were trying to recreate the French cheese, Neufchâtel.

Fudge Pie

Michael W. Terrio—Terrio's Carriage House, Schroon Lake

8 EGGS
4 cups SUGAR
6 squares BITTER CHOCOLATE, melted
2 cups chopped NUTS
2 tsp. VANILLA
2/3 cup MARGARINE, melted
2 (9-inch) unbaked PIE SHELLS

In a mixing bowl, beat eggs until foamy, adding sugar gradually; blend well. Add chocolate, nuts, vanilla and margarine. Stir thoroughly. Pour mixture into pie shells. Place in a 350° oven and bake for 35-40 minutes. Do not overbake, as pie should be moist. Glass pie plates are best for baking this pie. Serve with whipped cream or ice cream.

Schroon Lake

Schroon Lake is a resort community nestled in the Adirondack Mountains. Many outdoor recreational activities abound, including golf, tennis, hiking, biking, swimming, canoeing, sailing and fishing. One of the largest Ice Fishing Derbies in the Adirondack region is held here.

Biscuit Tortoni

3/4 cup dry MACAROON CRUMBS, divided
3/4 cup MILK
1/4 cup SUGAR
Pinch of SALT
2 cups WHIPPED CREAM
1/4 tsp. VANILLA
1/4 tsp. ALMOND EXTRACT

In a mixing bowl, soak 1/2 cup of macaroon crumbs with milk, sugar and salt for 1 hour. Fold in whipped cream. Add flavorings. Pour into 4 individual containers. Top with remaining crumbs. Freeze before serving.

★ ★ ★ ★ *Cooking Across America* ★ ★ ★ ★

Biscotti Banquet

"I make these for a local gourmet coffee shop. They are very popular with the customers!"

Wanda G. Dean—Wellsville

4 EGGS	2 tsp. VANILLA
1 1/2 cups SUGAR	3 tsp. BAKING POWDER
3/4 cup CANOLA OIL	1 1/2 tsp. SALT
or melted BUTTER	3 1/4 cups FLOUR

Whisk together in a bowl, eggs, sugar, oil and vanilla. Add dry ingredients and mix thoroughly. Place dough on a lightly-floured board and form into a ball. If not firm enough, add 1 or 2 additional tablespoons of flour. Slice ball in half. Roll out each half with lightly-floured hands into a log that is 12-14 inches long and 2 inches around. Place rolls on waxed paper and roll to cover. Refrigerate for 30 minutes. Remove from refrigerator and place on a baking sheet. Bake at 350° for 20 minutes or until lightly browned. Remove from oven and gently slide onto bread board. Let cool for 10 minutes. Using a sharp knife, slice diagonally into 3/4-inch slices. Place each slice on a baking sheet and bake for 15-20 minutes. Remove from oven and sprinkle with **POWDERED SUGAR.**

Variations: Just before adding dry ingredients to biscotti mixture, add your choice of the following:

Lemon-Poppy Seed Biscotti

Grated peel of 1 lemon, 2 tablespoons lemon juice and 2 tablespoons poppy seeds.

Orange Pistachio Biscotti

Grated peel of 1 orange, 2 tablespoons orange juice, 1 cup pistachios, 2 teaspoons ginger and 1 teaspoon almond extract.

Lemon-Anise Biscotti

1 tablespoon grated lemon peel, 2 teaspoons anise seed, 2 teaspoons lemon juice and 1 cup toasted, chopped walnuts or almonds.

Almond Biscotti

1/3 cup cherry brandy, 2 teaspoons almond flavoring, 1 2/3 cups slivered, toasted almonds.

 *Desserts*

A Victorian Sweet Secret

"The half-moon shape of these pies is common in the South, where my mother grew up. These could be deep fried, but I prefer to bake them."

Rosemary Barone—A Victorian on the Bay Bed & Breakfast,
Eastport

4 (9-inch) unbaked PIE SHELLS	3/4 cup BUTTER, softened
1 pkg. (8 oz.) CREAM CHEESE, softened	1/2 cup SHREDDED COCONUT
1 cup packed BROWN SUGAR	1/2 cup BUTTER, melted
1/4 cup POWDERED SUGAR	1/2 cup SUGAR
1 cup chopped PECANS	2 tsp. CINNAMON

Preheat oven to 350°. Cut pie shells into 4-inch circles. In a bowl, mix together next six ingredients. Place one heaping teaspoon of mixture in the center of each circle. Fold pie crust in half (half-moon shape) and seal edges with tines of fork. Place "pies" on a cookie sheet and bake at 350° for 10 minutes. While still warm, brush 1/2 cup butter lightly over tops of crusts. In a bowl, combine sugar and cinnamon and sprinkle over all. Return to oven for an additional 2 minutes.

Chocolate Crunch Muffins

"I am always looking for something different for my customers. They really like these...they are more like a dessert than a regular muffin."

Sherrie Young—Cakes by Sherrie, Tannersville

2 cups FLOUR	1/2 cup HEATH® ENGLISH TOFFEE BITS
1/2 cup SUGAR	
3 tsp. BAKING POWDER	2 EGGS
1/3 cup COCOA	2/3 cup APPLESAUCE

Combine dry ingredients in a bowl. Add remaining ingredients and blend. Pour mixture into lined muffin cups and bake at 400° for 5 minutes. Reduce heat to 375° and bake for an additional 20 minutes.

Autumn Maple Cake

Joyce Bordeau—Guilderland

1 1/2 cups FLOUR	1/2 cup SUGAR
1 tsp. BAKING POWDER	1/2 cup PURE MAPLE SYRUP
1/2 tsp. BAKING SODA	1/2 cup RAISINS
1/4 tsp. SALT	1/3 cup APPLESAUCE
1 EGG, beaten	1/3 cup COOKING OIL
1 1/2 cups peeled and chopped BAKING APPLES	1 1/2 tsp. grated ORANGE PEEL

Spray an 8 x 8 baking pan with cooking spray. In a mixing bowl, combine flour, baking powder, baking soda and salt. In a large mixing bowl, combine egg and apples. Stir in sugar, maple syrup, raisins, applesauce, oil and orange peel. Add dry ingredients and stir just until combined. Spread batter in prepared pan. Bake at 350° for 40-45 minutes or until a toothpick inserted in the center comes out clean. Brush warm cake with additional maple syrup and cool slightly. Serve with *Maple Cream Topping*.

Serves 8.

Maple Cream Topping

1/2 cup WHIPPING CREAM	1/4 cup PURE MAPLE SYRUP
1/2 cup SOUR CREAM	

Chill a bowl and electric mixer beaters. Add whipping cream to bowl and whip at medium speed until stiff peaks form. In a separate bowl, stir together sour cream and maple syrup. Fold into whipped cream. Spread on top of cake and serve immediately.

Welcome to America!

Between 1892 and 1924, Ellis Island processed twelve million immigrants. A recently established internet website: ellisislandrecords.org, allows you to research immigrants who arrived here during that period.

Frozen Custard

Whether made in your ice cream maker or freezer, this is a special treat for any occasion.

4 EGG YOLKS   **1 tsp. VANILLA EXTRACT**
1/3 cup SUGAR   **1/4 tsp. SALT**
1 1/2 cups LIGHT CREAM

In top half of a double boiler, beat egg yolks and sugar until light, thick and smooth. In a saucepan, scald cream; stir in vanilla and salt. Pour cream mixture into egg mixture, blending thoroughly as the cream is added. Add water to the bottom half of double boiler and bring to a simmer. Place top half of double boiler with egg mixture in it over simmering water. Using a wooden spoon, stir slowly and continually for 12 minutes or until custard is thick enough to coat the back of the spoon. Do not allow water to boil. Remove from heat and set pan in cold water. Cool to room temperature.

• **Ice Cream Maker Method:** Pour custard mixture into the ice cream canister and then freeze in ice cream maker according to the manufacturer's directions.

• **Manual/Freezer Method:** Pour custard mixture into several undivided ice cube trays. Cover and freeze until firm (3-6 hours). Using a fork, beat custard 3-4 times while freezing. Move to refrigerator 15 minutes before serving to soften.

The Chautauqua-Allegheny Region

The Chautauqua-Allegheny region in Western New York has been one of the nation's most popular vacation destinations for more than a century. The region is home to Allegheny State Park and many Amish and Native American communities. Lake Erie State Park and Lake Chautauqua State Park are two of the region's most popular vacation stops. Each year, many flock to the Busti Apple Harvest Festival.

Zeppoles

"This is a classic Italian dessert."

Jean Mulligan—Bethpage

2 EGGS
1 cup MILK
1 tsp. VANILLA
2 cups FLOUR

1 tsp. BAKING POWDER
OIL for frying
POWDERED SUGAR

In a bowl, mix eggs with milk and vanilla. In another bowl, blend flour and baking powder with a fork. Add egg mixture and blend well. Heat oil in a deep fryer and drop batter by rounded teaspoons into hot oil. Fry until puffed and browned on all sides. Drain on paper towels. Sprinkle with powdered sugar.

Apricot Mousse

Wagner Vineyards & Ginny Lee Café—Lodi

1 tsp. UNFLAVORED GELATIN
3/4 cup APRICOT PRESERVES
3/4 cup ORANGE JUICE
2 Tbsp. WAGNER'S® JOHANNISBERG RIESLING ICE WINE
2 cups WHIPPED TOPPING
MINT LEAVES

Sprinkle gelatin over apricot preserves in a small saucepan. Let stand 1 minute. Cook over low heat, stirring until gelatin dissolves, about 2 minutes. Add orange juice. Continue cooking over low heat for 2-3 minutes. Transfer to a large bowl. Add wine, stirring well. Cover and chill for 25 minutes or until mixture is the consistency of unbeaten egg whites. Beat gelatin mixture at high speed until light and fluffy. Cover and chill for 20 minutes. Gently fold in whipped topping, reserving a small amount for garnish. Chill at least 2 hours. Serve in champagne flutes or wine glasses. Top with a dollop of whipped cream and garnish with a mint leaf. Serve with Wagner's Johannisberg Riesling Ice Wine.

Serves 6-8.

Concord Grape Pie

In the Finger Lakes region of New York, Concord grapes come in during the first two weeks of September.

4 cups CONCORD GRAPES
1/2 cup SUGAR
1 1/2 Tbsp. LEMON JUICE

1 Tbsp. QUICK-COOKING
   TAPIOCA
PIE DOUGH for a 2 crust pie

Squeeze grapes to separate pulp and skin. Place pulps in a saucepan and skins in a bowl. Cook pulps until seeds loosen (10 minutes on medium heat). Press pulps through a colander to remove seeds. In a bowl, combine pulps, skins, sugar, lemon juice and tapioca. Let mixture stand for 15 minutes. Preheat oven to 450°. Line pie pan with pie dough, add grape mixture and then add top or create a lattice top. Bake for 10 minutes at 450°, then reduce heat to 350° and bake 20 minutes longer.

The New York State Canal System

The New York State Canal System links the Great Lakes with hundreds of miles of lakes and rivers from Buffalo to Albany. From Albany you can travel south on the Hudson to New York City or north to Lake Champlain. The Erie Canal and its linking canals, the Oswego, Cayuga-Seneca and Champlain, comprise a 542-mile canal system, connecting nearly every major city in New York.

Norwegian Apple Pie

Ontario Orchards of Oswego—Oswego

2 cups chopped APPLES
1 tsp. VANILLA
1 cup finely chopped WALNUTS
1 1/2 cups SUGAR
1 cup FLOUR

2 tsp. BAKING POWDER
Dash of SALT
2 EGGS
WHIPPED CREAM or
   ICE CREAM

In a bowl, mix together apples, vanilla and walnuts. Add remaining ingredients except whipped cream and mix well. Divide batter between 2 greased 9-inch glass pie plates. Bake for 30 minutes at 350°. Serve topped with whipped cream.

Strawberry Napoleons

Dorothy Berman—Queens

8 sheets PHYLLO DOUGH, thawed according to pkg. directions
3 cups PASTRY CREAM, at room temperature
3 cups sliced STRAWBERRIES
POWDERED SUGAR, for dusting

Preheat oven to 350°. Spray a baking sheet with nonstick vegetable spray. Spray a sheet of the phyllo dough with nonstick spray, fold in half and spray again, then fold once more and spray again. Cut the folded dough in quarters to make four even rectangles. Cut each rectangle in half. Repeat the process with the remaining sheets of phyllo. Place the rectangles on the baking sheet and bake until lightly browned, 3 to 4 minutes. Watch carefully, as they burn easily. For each napoleon, spread three of the rectangles with 1 tablespoon of *Pastry Cream*, then 1 tablespoon of the berries. Stack the three layers, then top with the remaining rectangle. Lightly dust with powdered sugar. Repeat until all napoleons have been assembled.

Makes 16 napoleons.

Pastry Cream

3 cups LOW FAT MILK   **4 Tbsp. CORNSTARCH**
2/3 cup SUGAR   **1 1/2 Tbsp. VANILLA**
2 WHOLE EGGS & 1 EGG YOLK

Using double boiler, heat 2 1/2 cups milk until steam rises from the surface. In a separate bowl, whisk together eggs, remaining 1/2 cup milk and sugar. Sift in cornstarch and whisk until well-blended. Remove from heat and gradually whisk in egg mixture. Return pan to top of double boiler and whisk constantly over medium heat until thickened and smooth, about 5 minutes. Remove from heat and stir in vanilla. Transfer to bowl, press plastic wrap onto pastry cream surface, and refrigerate until ready to use. Can be stored for up to 3 days.

Half-Moon Cookies

Not to be confused with a Black-and-White cookie, these are an upstate New York favorite!

1 cup MILK	1/2 tsp. SALT
1 Tbsp. WHITE VINEGAR	3 cups FLOUR
1 1/2 cups SUGAR	1 tsp. BAKING POWDER
3/4 cup SHORTENING	1 tsp. BAKING SODA
2 EGGS	1 tsp. VANILLA

Preheat oven to 375°. In a bowl, combine milk and vinegar; let sit for 5 minutes. In a large bowl, cream together sugar and shortening. Add eggs and beat thoroughly. In another bowl, sift together flour, baking powder and salt. Stir baking soda into milk mixture, then blend it into the creamed mixture, alternating with flour mixture. Stir in vanilla. Drop by tablespoon onto an ungreased cookie sheet. Bake for 10 minutes, then remove to rack to cool. When cooled, turn cookies upside down and frost half of the bottom with *Chocolate Frosting* and the other half with *Vanilla Frosting*.

Chocolate-Coffee Frosting

3 cups POWDERED SUGAR	3 Tbsp. melted BUTTER
3 Tbsp. STRONG COFFEE	1 tsp. VANILLA
4 Tbsp. COCOA	

In a bowl, combine all ingredients.

Vanilla Frosting

3 Tbsp. melted BUTTER	3 Tbsp. MILK
3 cups POWDERED SUGAR	2 tsp. VANILLA

In a bowl, combine all ingredients.

Did You Know?
New York is the third largest dairy state in America!

Graham Streusel Cake with Vanilla Glaze

Ethel Miller—Averill Park

2 cups GRAHAM CRACKER CRUMBS
3/4 cup chopped NUTS
3/4 cup packed BROWN SUGAR
1 tsp. CINNAMON
3/4 cup BUTTER or MARGARINE, melted
1 pkg. (18.25 oz.) CAKE MIX, any flavor
1 cup WATER
1/4 cup OIL
3 EGGS

Preheat oven to 350°. Grease and flour a 13 x 9 baking pan. In a bowl, combine graham cracker crumbs, nuts, brown sugar, cinnamon and butter. In a large bowl, with mixer on low speed, blend together cake mix, water, oil and eggs until moistened. Pour 1/2 of the batter into baking pan. Sprinkle with 1/2 of graham cracker mixture and spread remaining batter evenly over top. Sprinkle with remaining graham cracker mixture. Bake for 45-50 minutes until a toothpick inserted in center comes out clean. Drizzle cake with *Vanilla Glaze.*

Vanilla Glaze

1 cup POWDERED SUGAR   1-2 Tbsp. WATER
1 tsp. VANILLA

Mix sugar, vanilla and water together until smooth.

Lake Placid

Having hosted the 1932 and 1980 Winter Olympic Games, Lake Placid has become a world-renowned tourist destination. The town, which offers year-round sporting events including ice skating and horse shows, draws many to its Winter Olympic Museum.

Garden Fresh Apple Pie

"This filling can also be used as a topping."

Ali Dorian—*New York New Wave Health Recipes,* Staten Island

6 lg. APPLES, peeled and sliced
1/2 cup RAISINS (soaked overnight in water or juice)
JUICE of 2 lg. LEMONS
1/2 Tbsp. APPLE PIE SPICE or CINNAMON
1 Tbsp. HONEY
1/4 tsp. SEA SALT

In a large bowl, mix all ingredients until well-blended. Pour into **No-Bake Pie Crust** and serve.

No-Bake Pie Crust

1 1/2 cups chopped WALNUTS
3/4 cup raw or lightly toasted WHEAT GERM
1 tsp. CINNAMON
2 tsp. HONEY
3 Tbsp. SOY MARGARINE

In a blender or food processor, mix walnuts, wheat germ, cinnamon and honey. Cut in margarine and mix well. Chill for 30 minutes. Press into an 8-inch pie plate.

Lemon Ices

A favorite of New Yorkers!

2 cups WATER
1 cup SUGAR
1 cup LEMON JUICE

Combine water and sugar in a saucepan and bring to a boil over high heat, stirring just until sugar is dissolved. Boil, uncovered, for 5 minutes; remove from heat and allow to cool to room temperature. Add lemon juice, stir and pour into a metal pan. Freeze for 3-4 hours, stirring every 30 minutes with a fork, scraping crystals from edge of pan. When finished, it should have a fine, crumbly texture, like coarse snow.

Frozen Fruit Squares

"This is a family favorite as well as a great dessert for church or other group dinners. Fresh blueberries, peaches, strawberries or raspberries—all grown locally in western New York state—make this an especially good dessert."

Mary Jane Reid—Home Baking, Almond

1/3 cup EGG WHITES	2 tsp. LEMON JUICE
1 cup SUGAR	1 cup HEAVY CREAM,
2 cups fresh BERRIES	WHIPPED

Beat egg whites with sugar, berries and lemon juice until thick. Fold whipped cream into fruit mixture. Spread 2/3 of crumbled *Brown Sugar Crust* in a 13 x 9 pan and top with fruit mixture. Sprinkle remaining crumbled crust over top; freeze for 6 hours or overnight. Cut into squares and serve.

Brown Sugar Crust

1/2 cup MARGARINE, melted	1/4 cup BROWN SUGAR
1/2 cup chopped WALNUTS	1 cup FLOUR

Combine all ingredients and spread on a cookie sheet. Bake at 350° for 20 minutes. Remove from oven and stir, breaking crust into crumbs.

Graham Cracker Fudge

"My mother shared this recipe with me many years ago."

Eileen Schunk—Eden

2 cups SUGAR	1 cup GRAHAM CRACKER
1 cup EVAPORATED MILK	CRUMBS
1/2 cup BUTTER	3/4 cup WALNUTS
1 cup CHOCOLATE CHIPS	1 tsp. VANILLA
3/4 cup FLOUR	

In a large saucepan, combine sugar, milk and butter. Boil for 10 minutes. Add remaining ingredients to mixture and mix well. Pour into an 8 x 8 pan. Cool and cut into squares.

Cream Cheese Cookies

"This is one of my mother's special recipes!"

Susan Thrasher—Clifton Park

1 pkg. (8 oz.) CREAM CHEESE
1 cup MARGARINE
2 1/4 cups FLOUR
2 cups CHOCOLATE CHIPS

1 can (14 oz.) SWEETENED
  CONDENSED MILK
1 cup chopped NUTS
POWDERED SUGAR

Soften cream cheese and margarine, then combine with flour to make dough; refrigerate overnight. Place chocolate chips in a double boiler, add milk and allow chips to melt; add nuts. Sprinkle work area with a small amount of powdered sugar and roll dough out to 1/4-inch thickness. Spread with chocolate mixture. Roll up jelly roll style, slice into 1/2-inch pieces and place on an ungreased cookie sheet. Bake at 350° until edges turn brown.

Applesauce Nougat Cookies

Esther LaClair—LaFayette Apple Festival, LaFayette

2 cups FLOUR
1/2 tsp. SALT
1/2 tsp. CINNAMON
1/2 tsp. NUTMEG
1/2 tsp. CLOVES
1/2 tsp. ALLSPICE
1/2 cup SHORTENING

1 cup packed BROWN SUGAR
1 tsp. BAKING SODA
1 cup APPLESAUCE
1 EGG, well-beaten
1 pkg. (6 oz.) CHOCOLATE
  CHIPS
1 cup broken WALNUTS

Preheat oven to 375°. In a bowl, sift together flour, salt and spices. In another bowl, cream together shortening and sugar. In a third bowl, combine baking soda, applesauce and egg. Blend applesauce and creamed mixtures. Add dry ingredients. Stir in chocolate chips and nuts. Drop by teaspoons onto a greased baking sheet 2-3 inches apart. Bake for 12-15 minutes.

New York Food Festival Sampler

May—Maple Festival—Croghan. **Food Tour of Italy**—Hammondsport. **International Food Festival**—New York City. **Hudson River Festival & Shad Bake**—Orangetown. **Dutch Festival**—Uniondale.

June—Bavarian Festival—Round Top. **Strawberry Festival**—Livingston Manor. **Old-Fashioned Strawberry Festival**—Schoharie. **Merritt Estate Winery Strawberry Festival**—Forestville. **Strawberry Festival**—Ovid. **Strawberry Festival**—Oswego. **Strawberry Festival**—Wolcott. **Strawberry Extravaganza**—Gasport. **Strawberry Fest**—Youngstown. **Strawberry Festival**—Albion. **Greek Food Festival**—West Nyack. **Hudson Valley Wine & Food Festival**—Annandale-On-Hudson. **Strawberry Festival**—Wingdale. **Strawberry Festival**—Beacon. **Strawberry Festival**—Mattituck.

July—Raspberry Festival—Binghamton. **Italian Heritage & Food Festival**—Buffalo. **Raspberry Jamboree**—Gasport. **Taste of Buffalo**—Buffalo. **Bounty of the Hudson**—Warwick. **International Food & Music Festival**—Poughkeepsie.

August—Taste of Ellicottville—Ellicottville. **Harvest Festival**—Dansville. **Potato Festival**—Wayland. **Sauerkraut Festival**—Phelps. **The Great New York State Chili Championship**—Oswego. **Potluck Food & Music Festival**—Buffalo. **Bertolli Culinary Festival**—Tarrytown. **Vineyard Wine & Food Festival**—North Salem. **Taste of Oswego**—Oswego.

September—Taste of the North Country—Glens Falls. **Hunter Mountain Microbrew, Wine and Fine Foods Festival**—Hunter. **Applefest**—Fly Creek. **Busti Apple Festival**—Jamestown. **Merritt Estate Winery Septemberfest**—Forestville. **Corn Festival**—Cincinnatus. **Leaves and Lobsters on the Lawn**—Dundee. **Potato Festival**—Richford. **Tomato Fest of CNY**—Auburn. **Italian Festival**—Holley. **Apple Festival**—Hopewell Junction. **Hudson Valley Garlic Festival**—Saugerties. **Lobsterfest**—New Paltz. **Taste of New Paltz**—New Paltz. **Apple Festival**—Central Square.

October—Apple Festival—Croghan. **Apple Festival**—Newark Valley. **Apple Harvest Festival**—Ithaca. **Grape-Pumpkin Festival**—Hammondsport. **Great Cortland Pumpkinfest**—Cortland. **Apple Festival**—Lafayette. **Apple & Pumpkin Fest**—Waterport. **Pumpkin Festival**—Red Hook. **Applefest**—Warwick. **Oyster Festival**—Oyster Bay. **Pumpkin Fest**—Yaphank.

November—International Pickle Festival—Rosendale.

INDEX

Index (continued)

Index (continued)

New York Cook Book Contributors

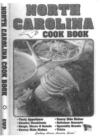

NORTH CAROLINA COOK BOOK

Filled with family favorites as well as recipes that showcase North Carolina's specialty foods. *Sausage Pinwheels, Shipwrecked Crab, Scuppernong Grape Butter, Carolina Blender Slaw, North Carolina Pork BBQ, Rock Fish Muddle, Hushpuppy Fritters, Hummingbird Cake, Peanut Butter Pie!*
5 1/2 x 8 1/2 — 96 pages . . . $6.95

FLORIDA COOK BOOK

Great recipes from the Sunshine State! Sample *Mango-Champagne Fritters* or *Baked Cheese Papaya, Ham-Tomato Quiche, Florida Blueberry Streusel Coffee Cake, Sautéed Gulf Coast Grouper, Crab & Cheese Pie* or *Drunken Shrimp.* Special Florida seafood section, tasty side dishes and delightful desserts. Includes fascinating facts and trivia.
5 1/2 x 8 1/2 — 96 pages . . . $6.95

VIRGINIA COOK BOOK

Over 140 recipes from all across this great state! From unbeatable seafood recipes to savory ham dishes, crab specialties, delicious apple recipes, tempting peanut delights and a cornucopia of historical and family favorites. Includes Virginia facts and trivia.
5 1/2 x 8 1/2 — 96 pages . . . $6.95

INDIANA COOK BOOK

Straight from the heart of the Hoosier State! Try a *Kielbasa Appetizer, Blue Cheese Mushrooms, Grandmother Reagan's Waffles, Amish Acres Bean Soup, Pork Steaks with Sour Cream Salsa, Baked Sauerkraut, Acorn-Cranberry Squash, Blueberry Pizza* and many more. Includes facts and trivia.
5 1/2 x 8 1/2 — 96 pages . . . $6.95

ILLINOIS COOK BOOK

Enjoy the flavors of Illinois! Over 100 recipes that celebrate Illinois. *Reuben in the Round, Pork Medallions in Herb Sauce, Autumn's Swiss Supper, Carrot Soufflé, Sky High Honey Biscuits, Rhubarb Cream Pie* to name just a few. Includes fascinating facts and trivia.
5 1/2 x 8 1/2 — 96 pages . . . $6.95

More Cook Books from Golden West Publishers

APPLE LOVERS COOK BOOK

Celebrating America's favorite—the apple! 150 recipes for main and side dishes, appetizers, salads, breads, muffins, cakes, pies, desserts, beverages, and preserves, all kitchen-tested by Shirley Munson and Jo Nelson.

5 1/2 x 8 1/2 — 120 Pages . . . $6.95

BERRY LOVERS COOK BOOK

Berrylicious recipes for enjoying these natural wonders. From *Blueberry Muffins, Strawberry Cheesecake* and *Raspberry Sticky Rolls* to *Boysenberry Mint Frosty* or *Gooseberry Crunch,* you will find tasty recipes that will bring raves from your friends and family. Includes berry facts and trivia.

5 1/2 x 8 1/2 — 96 Pages . . . $6.95

SEAFOOD LOVERS COOK BOOK

Recipes from coast to coast! Presenting lobster, crab, oysters, clams, salmon, swordfish, tuna, grouper, halibut and many more, featured in appetizers, soups, salads, side and main dishes. Includes seafood tips and trivia.

5 1/2 x 8 1/2 — 96 Pages . . . $6.95

SALSA LOVERS COOK BOOK

More than 180 taste-tempting recipes for salsas that will make every meal a special event! Salsas for salads, appetizers, main dishes and desserts! Put some salsa in your life! More than 200,000 copies in print!

5 1/2 x 8 1/2—128 pages . . . $6.95

VEGGIE LOVERS COOK BOOK

Everyone will love these no-cholesterol, no-animal recipes! Over 200 nutritious, flavorful recipes by Chef Morty Star. Includes a foreword by Dr. Michael Klaper. Nutritional analysis for each recipe to help you plan a healthy diet.

5 1/2 x 8 1/2 — 128 pages . . . $6.95

ORDER BLANK

GOLDEN WEST PUBLISHERS

☼ 4113 N. Longview Ave. • Phoenix, AZ 85014

www.goldenwestpublishers.com • **1-800-658-5830** • FAX 602-279-6901

Qty	Title	Price	Amount
	Apple Lovers Cook Book	6.95	
	Bean Lovers Cook Book	6.95	
	Berry Lovers Cook Book	6.95	
	Chili-Lovers' Cook Book	6.95	
	Chip and Dip Lovers Cook Book	6.95	
	Corn Lovers Cook Book	6.95	
	Easy RV Recipes	6.95	
	Easy Recipes for Wild Game & Fish	6.95	
	Florida Cook Book	6.95	
	Illinois Cook Book	6.95	
	Indiana Cook Book	6.95	
	Joy of Muffins	6.95	
	Mexican Desserts and Drinks	6.95	
	New York Cook Book	6.95	
	North Carolina Cook Book	6.95	
	Pennsylvania Cook Book	6.95	
	Salsa Lovers Cook Book	6.95	
	Seafood Lovers Cook Book	6.95	
	Veggie Lovers Cook Book	6.95	
	Virginia Cook Book	6.95	

Shipping & Handling Add: United States $4.00
Canada & Mexico $5.00—All others $12.00

☐ My Check or Money Order Enclosed

☐ MasterCard ☐ VISA

Total $ _____

(Payable in U.S. funds)

Acct. No. _____ Exp. Date _____

Signature _____

Name _____ Phone _____

Address _____

City/State/Zip _____

Call for a FREE catalog of all of our titles

This order blank may be photo copied.

9/03

NY Ck Bk